God's People Without God's Word

TOWERING
BABBLE

God's People Without God's Word

TOWERING BABBLE

Vernard Eller

The Brethren Press
Elgin, Illinois

TOWERING BABBLE

By the kind permission of the Wm. B. Eerdmans Publishing Company, the following materials are used in this book: (1) In Chapter Four the Blumhardt quotations are from Vernard Eller (Ed.), *Thy Kingdom Come: A Blumhardt Reader.* (2) Chapter Six has constant reference to Markus Barth, *Justification.* (3) Chapter Eight quotes extensively from Karl Barth, *The Christian Life.*

Cover design by Kathy Kline

Library of Congress Cataloging in Publication Data

Eller, Vernard.
    Towering babble.

    1. Church of the Brethren—Doctrinal and controversial works. 2. Theology. I. Title.
BX7821.2.E43   1983   289.7′3   83-4621
ISBN 0-87178-855-1

Printed in the United States of America
by The Brethren Press, Elgin, Ill.

TO THE BRETHREN OF THE PACIFIC SLOPE

who have acted toward me, from the day of my birth,
as nursing mothers in the Lord,
as my classmates and counselors at college,
as my students and colleagues at the same college,
as co-workers in the church,
as hosts for my visits,
as putter-uppers with my ideas,
and as sometime putter-downers of the same —
all in wonderful patience, kindness, and love.

For what you have been to me, I thank you —
and I thank the Lord!

VERNARD

Contents

Introduction

Some people may think this book too narrow, focusing, as it does, entirely on the Church of the Brethren. Yet, narrow focus is in no way the intent. There is no question but that it could as well have been written with a focus upon any of the so-called "mainline" churches (say, members of the National Council of Churches); and on certain points it will be accurate regarding even the so-called "evangelical" churches. A broad spectrum of readers will have no difficulty in applying the critique to a broad spectrum of churches; and the desire behind the book is that it be so applied.

Nevertheless, I deliberately chose not to shotgun my charges all over the place, banging away at the Methodists on one point, the Episcopalians on another, the Presbyterians on another, and the Brethren only once in awhile. That would have been too easy, would have had the effect only of weakening my case, would have given an out for churches to defend themselves by pointing at parties more guilty than they. So the Church of the Brethren is here presented as a "case study"—which is to say that its situation, rather than being in any way exceptional, is sadly typical. Thus, my hope is that the reader will not say, "Wouldn't you know? Those Brethren are a bad lot," but rather, "If this is the way it is with the Brethren, there must be many other churches just as bad off—and perhaps some that are even worse!" This book is not meant as an "in house" conversation but as addressing a wide audience.

Yet, it must be quickly admitted that the choice of the Church of the Brethren for my "case study" was not a random or arbitrary decision. It certainly was not my thought that the Brethren would make the *best* example by being the *worst* of the lot; I do not for a moment believe that to be true. A professionally-conducted sociological study of church life in Canada, reported in *Christianity Today* [Feb. 19, '82, p. 28], concluded that only one of every seven members of the United Church of Canada can be said to be committed to historic, biblical Christianity. Yet, I would never suggest that the Church of the Brethren has come to such a state.

No, I have made the Church of the Brethren my case simply because it is the denomination I know best. I have served in its ordained ministry for over thirty years now, have preached and taught in its congregations, camps, and conferences across the land. I have held office on all levels of its denominational structure, have been a functionary on its national staff, a professor in one of its colleges, and a member of its governing board. I can speak with more authority regarding the Church of the Brethren than years of research would enable me to do regarding any other denomination.

But more, I have chosen the Church of the Brethren because, frankly, I *care* about it more than I do any other denomination. Of course, I am sad to see any group drifting away from its historic commitment. But if I can say or do anything to help my own church counter such drift, that, above all, is my deepest and most heartfelt desire (regarding not only this book but my ministry as a whole). Yet, while attempting that, I also am eager to have other Christians read the book for whatever help it can be in their situations. Thus, at every point, I will give sufficient explanation to make my Brethren references comprehensible to "outsiders."

Some people may feel the book is too narrow in speaking, as it does, to just one point, bringing only one accusation and never varying from 'it. Yes, it is true that my charge could have been as shotgun in this respect as in its shooting at many churches. But again, my desire is not to be narrow but to be powerful. I could talk about "heresy" or "apostasy" — if those were terms that any longer had meaning. I could accuse the church of deserting "orthodoxy," the classic creeds and confessions of Christendom, its own historic tradition. I could accuse it of "false teaching," of being unfaithful toward God and Jesus Christ. I could accuse it of rejecting the guidance of the Holy Spirit. I could speak of people defecting on their baptismal and ordination vows. My accusation could be made multifarious, worded in any number of different ways.

However, my decision is to apply the pressure and keep the

argument centered—this by insisting only that the church is defaulting on its commitment to the New Testament as its rule of faith and practice. This is the one indictment the Church of the Brethren will have the most difficulty in wriggling out of. The idea—if not the exact wording—goes back to the church's founding in 1708. The wording itself goes back a good long way and has been constantly reaffirmed throughout the life of the denomination. In 1979, as part of a major paper regarding the inspiration of scripture, the delegate body of the Annual Conference (made up of representatives from all the congregations and districts, and itself the highest authority within the church) solemnly reiterated the statement. In 1981, then, although without quite the same self-conscious deliberation, that statement was passed once more, as part of a paper on the diminishing membership of the denomination. And most recently, in 1982, Conference spoke of our "confidence that the scriptures are 'the infallible rule of faith and practice'"—this is in a paper, "A Vision of Unity in the Church of the Brethren in the 1980's."

And what is most significant (or damning, as the case may be) is the fact that, to my knowledge, there has never been any expressed dissent to this commitment. Whenever it is proposed that the New Testament is our rule of faith and practice, the Brethren not only pass the motion, they pass it unanimously and without any other possibility even coming into consideration. So if it can be shown—as this book now proposes to do—that within contemporary Brethren faith and practice there is a great deal that actually violates the New Testament rule, the very pointed question can be put, "Why does a segment of the membership keep voting for that commitment if it has no intention of taking it seriously?" Or, to put the matter conversely, "If you think the New Testament ought not be taken as our rule of faith and practice, why are you unwilling to propound and argue that position within the councils of the church?" And it is to the end of holding the nose of the church right to that spot that I have chosen to raise no other issue. Non-Brethren readers whose churches are not founded on quite the same commitment certainly will be able to reword the concern to fit their own situations.

I hope it will be clear that I am not suggesting the existence of some sort of plot or any malicious intent aimed at undercutting the biblical base of the church. That, rather plainly, is not what has happened. There is no evidence of plotting. No Brethren have invented or even given much in the way of leadership regarding the unbiblical ideas this book will uncover. Rather, we have simply been careless about another church commitment — this one having to do with not being conformed to the world. Consequently, we have been seduced by unbiblical elements within the greater church around us, within the currents of theological scholarship, within the fashions of secular culture. Yet none of this, of course, is an excuse for our voting one way while practicing another, for failing to put our moneys (and everything else we have and are) where our mouths are.

Some people may find this book too *negative* in its radical criticism of the church and some of the leaders of the church. But the intention is that the book be read as altogether positive. Note specifically that, for every charge of unbiblicalness that is brought, there is deliberately proposed a truly biblical alternative — for every negative accusation, a positive witness of scripture. In addition, my purpose in the writing of the book is truly positive. Certainly it can be nothing but positive for the church to get honest with itself: "honest," first, in facing the truth about its position in respect to its own solemn profession; and "honest," next, in being pointed back and then in getting back to where God would have it be and where the church itself says it wants to be. Read as intended, the book is positive.

As will be recounted in the next chapter, this book was triggered by a specific event, the 1981 Church of the Brethren Annual Conference held in Indianapolis, Indiana. That conference put the burden on my heart — or at least convinced me that I had to speak out. It did not, at that point, tell me I had a book; that had to come by stages.

A month or so after Conference, I was a leader at a family camp of the Oregon-Washington District (Church of the Brethren) at its Camp Koinonia. I spoke three times; and those three addresses became the nuclei of what you will now read as Chapters Three, Four, and Six (Chapter Five thrust itself in long after everything else had been completed). But what has wound up as Chapter Six—the treatment of *exhomologesis,* which may be the most crucial idea in the book—on the way to becoming a chapter has also taken the form of an address to an interfaith banquet, a church school lesson at the Pacific Southwest Conference (California and Arizona Church of the Brethren) district meeting, and a sermon preached before both Brethren and non-Brethren audiences.

Chapter Two—on Micah 6:8—came to birth a month or so after Koinonia, when I was asked to lead a study of our denominational slogan with the young people at that PSWC district meeting. Following that trial run, I wrote up my notes as a chapter for this book, also submitting it as an article for the Church of the Brethren MESSENGER. An abridged version consequently appeared there.

Chapter Seven—on the theology of justice—was a late bloomer. It originated the next May, as a Bible study I conducted as part of a denominational stewardship seminar sponsored for Brethren congregations in the state of Oregon. Since being put into chapter form, it has been used in a congregational study group, as a paper at a meeting of the Society of Christian Ethics, a course of study for area Methodists, and a lecture series at Augustana College.

The remaining chapters, then, without warning, have come along one by one, each in its time, though each being written specifically for the book. Thus, although the completed work obviously is organized around a common theme, it did not originate with an overall plan—it just grew.

But the all-important conclusion is that the book should not and cannot be understood as though an outsider—or even an alienated or disenchanted member—was set on bringing down the Church of the Brethren. My own theological stance is nothing if not a *product* of that church; and my energies regularly have been expended in the *service* of that church. The book itself has evolved from give-and-take discussion *within* that body. There is nothing foreign here. And I mean the book for no other purpose than to encourage the Brethren (and as many others as care to) freely to examine their faith and practice among themselves. You are invited in. And may God both guide and bless us as we seek together to grow up into his truth.

CHAPTER ONE

Babble Up!

This chapter deals with the "architecture" of theology and is intent upon making the point that towers—and particularly Towers of Babel—almost always are built from below, i.e., from the ground up rather than from the top down. You will need to read further to discover the significance of this.

I have said that this book was "triggered" by the 1981 Indianapolis Annual Conference of the Church of the Brethren. That is not to say that that one conference is the issue with which the book is concerned. It was merely a symptom of what moved me to make this diagnosis. Clearly, Indianapolis was neither the beginning nor the end of the flood that is inundating the church. I don't even know that it is the high-water mark. I am using my experience of that conference to kick off this study; I have no desire that it dominate this study.

It would not be wrong to say that the whole of my ministry—teaching, preaching, and writing—has been intended as a counter and alternative to the theological position which only here finally gets named and identified. Nevertheless, for the sake of politeness and at least the appearance of unity within the church, I (along with the Brethren generally) to this point have refrained from specifying the "opposition," the position which stands over against my own, that which I see as the threat to biblical Brethrenism.

This is not a book I would ever have *wanted* to write. I personally have nothing to gain from it. It is bound to alienate many of my friends and colleagues. Every consideration of personal and professional advantage would say not to do it. So this is a reluctant book, done only out of an inner compulsion.

As suggested earlier, it comes to focus upon the fact that, since its beginning and right up to the present, a central commitment of the Church of the Brethren has been that the New Testament is its rule of faith and practice.

Now, in the context of that statement, the word "rule" must be understood as meaning — not so much "law" or "prescription" — as "standard, norm, measure, yardstick, plumbline." Yet if that be the case, it accomplishes absolutely nothing to keep saying that the New Testament is our rule unless we truly are using it as such, putting the biblical plumbline alongside the actuality of our faith and practice to see how they measure up. And I could not see that any plumblining of the sort was being done among us. In fact, there seems to be a tacit understanding that such shall not be done — it would amount to criticizing other people's faith statements, their sermons, worship services, prayers, hymns, litanies, or writings.

Of course, it would have to be admitted that our unwillingness to criticize has been very one-sided. Both the church leadership and our publications have felt very free to have at the faith and practice of "conservatives and fundamentalists," while not at all welcoming criticism in the reverse direction. Yet, surely the health of the body would dictate that, throughout the church, member be relating to member in the *mutual* discipline of plumblining the faith.

"I would like to talk to you about that sermon, Pastor. [Also, of course, talk by anyone to anyone about church school lesson, church magazine article, conference address, conversational statement, anything regarding our common faith.] But do you really feel the New Testament supports your interpretation? Let's talk about it."

And the sole purpose of this book is to initiate such theological/biblical discussion — this, in place of the polite but unhealthy silence that so little becomes a people who call themselves biblical. My interest is only in holding the Brethren to the rule they have freely claimed as their own. I want to help teach people how to properly use their plumbline. Especially in the Church of the Brethren, a primary responsibility of pastors and all other leaders should be in training the laity to apply the New Testament critically to any and every instance of faith or practice.

I hope it can be clear that I am not here presuming to act as owner or master of the rule; my judgments are not presented as being those of the Bible itself. I do have some qualifications and experience as a biblical theologian, but the book is meant to represent very much of a give-and-take. By the very nature of the case, the process must begin with my "giving." But I invite any and all readers to correct me where I have misunderstood the rule or applied it wrongly. The book is intended as a first word and definitely not the last word on the subject. It wants to be measured *by* the plumbline as well as do measuring *with* the plumbline. But in any case, it is imperative that the rule be taken out of the apron of our official proclamations and, for better or for worse, be put to use in measuring up the jerry-rigged structures of our faith and practice.

The following account of the Annual Conference that pushed me into this book will also stand as a first example of what the remainder of the book will be, a holding of the biblical plumbline alongside contemporary expressions of Brethrenism. Non-Brethren readers can make corresponding measurements for whatever ecclesiasticalities they care to measure. Yet, although much of today's "Brethrenism" is going to be "condemned" (in the same sense that a dangerously leaning building is condemned on the basis of plumbline measurements), I insist that my ultimate purpose is always positive. So consider that rules (plumblines) are not instruments used in wrecking buildings but in getting them strengthened, squared away, and right.

A Church of the Brethren Annual Conference is not constituted solely of voting delegates. Everyone is invited; and there are regularly more "everyones" present than there are delegates. And Conference is only partly business meetings; it is as much or more faith proclamation through preaching and worship. In what follows, I am speaking only of this second side of the Indianapolis Conference.

The theme was "Go Now with God"—obviously an effort to tie in with the final, "walk humbly" phrase of our denominational slogan from Micah 6:8 (see Chapter Two following). Thus the dictated move was to pick up on the biblical motif of a journey, or quest. Yet, as the conference transpired, it became apparent to me that we were not actually following the biblical model but another, namely, one from the contemporary psychology of religion. Let me try a summary description of the pattern that regularly came through the presentations of our own Brethren leaders (we also had a few guest speakers).

The journey presented for our consideration was that of the individual's "faith pilgrimage." Actually, this is to talk about a multiplicity of journeys, because there are as many as there are individuals, each journey uniquely one's own. In essence, each is the *inner* journey of my own religious experience—or in any case, my inner, religious response to the outward events of my personal history. The best and most typical expression of such journeying is undoubtedly the private journal, diary, or log.

At Conference, as in the literature of the subject, the term most prominently used in characterizing this quest is "pathos." Both the nature of the journey and the charting of it center predominantly in one's "feelings," in particular, one's feelings about oneself—"self-awareness," if you will. This is nothing if not an introspective and sentimental journey.

And most noteworthy is the fact that it is not the sort of journey to which any outside or public measures can be applied—as to whether the journey is a good one or a bad, whether it is headed in a right direction or a wrong one. It is not the sort of journey that has a predetermined destination in relation to which we might measure progression or retrogression. No, if I feel good about myself, then things are right with myself. The only sin is either the failure of courage to strike out into pathos or to be wandering through life unaware, without being in touch with myself. Indeed, the journey *is* the very exercise of self-awareness. Consequently, there is no question about *where* the quest is headed but only *how* courageously and feelingly the questor is questing.

But, we were told, if the questor will enter the pathos of the human condition boldly and deliberately, he has the assurance of encountering God. The word "destination" is probably too spatial and localized; but perhaps it would be correct to say that the "end" and "outcome" of the journey is God.

Now that end and outcome was also described in quite different terms as being the finding of self-identity, self-worth, self-fulfillment, authentic selfhood—as feeling good about oneself, as being liberated, as experiencing rightness.

The precise relationship between these two definitions of the journey's outcome was never made quite clear. Is God the transcendent being who, in his own freedom, encounters what person he chooses, to bestow on him the identity, the "rightness," that God himself deems right? Or is "God" a term used to identify and describe the character of the religious experience that comes to those who quest rightly? Is God Lord, or is he a creature of our faith-experience?

It was at this point in the exposition that some of the speakers tended to drop the word "God" in favor of such religion-terms as "the divine presence," "the numinous," "the holy." And that may be significant: (1) It could be a means of avoiding the use of personal pronouns for God—not having to call God "he" or "she." (2) It could be a way of depersonalizing God so as to steer entirely clear of implications that he, as Lord, might render any opinion of the questor or his journey. "Divine presences" aren't all that likely to take matters into their own hands, trying to exercise sovereignty, to make judgments or give orders—which, you can depend upon it, the biblical God will do every chance he gets. (3) It could be a way of getting "God" more nearly synonymous with religious experience itself and a particular state of consciousness.

But give the speakers the benefit of the doubt and make their "God" as biblical as you can, two things are still undeniable: (1) The journey is our human journey *to* God, rather than his journey to us or our journey *with* him (or a journey directed by him). And (2) God's function and value lies in the use he can be to the questor.

So here we have a contemporary, composite (i.e., constructed from the thought of several speakers) Brethren statement of faith—although the line of thought is very common today and in no way a particular creation of the Brethren. However, we are ready, now, to take out our rule and start measuring.

In the first place, the Bible would firmly resist the radical privatism and individualism of this definition of the journey. Especially under its journey metaphor, scripture insists on treating people in groups, as communities—always caravans, never flights of the alone to the Alone.

Likewise, the Bible would resist this plurality of journeys, each person on his own. In fact, it could be argued that all of the Bible's great journeys are to be understood as stages upon the one, all-encompassing journey from Creation to New Creation, from Eden to the New Jerusalem. The Epistle to the Hebrews is our best help here—the author bringing into the caravan every Old Testament character he can think of (Chapter 11) and then bringing in "us," along with Jesus Christ (Chapter 12). And he makes it clear that the whole shebang is headed toward "the city which has foundations, whose builder and maker is God." And notice, if you will, that, throughout scripture, the journey's end is regularly pictured in terms of *social* justice rather than *private* beatitude.

More, the site of biblical journeying has nothing to do with inner experience and feeling. Those are given any significance at all only as they produce "fruit." And fruit denotes outward, public, social, historical results. No, the happenings of history, rather than the experiences of interiority, form the pathway of biblical journeying.

It follows from this that biblical journeying always is open to judgment and always is being judged. The questors have an assigned destination and, at any given moment, are either on the right road or the wrong one, are either progressing or retrogressing, are either looking toward their destination or are looking everywhere but. The biblical journey has direction—and thus objective norms, standards, requirements, and disciplines of which inner questing knows nothing.

Again, in the Bible, God is never introduced simply at the end and outcome of the journey. He is also there as *Lord*—as the one who decides there shall be a journey; calls the questors to it; assigns them their roles within it; says when, where, and how things are to move; leads the way, makes a way, disciplines the wayward, even carries those who need to be carried when they need to be carried— and all to the destination he specifies. The journey is not a human journey *to* God; it is God's journey *with* us.

Likewise, the search for self-identity is no part of the biblical picture. Rather, at the outset, God *assigns* identities to people so that their subsequent journeying will have purpose and direction. "Abraham, you are to be father of a great nation in the land that I will show you. Let's go!" "Moses, my servant and leader of the Exodus. Let's go!" "Israel, you shall be my people, and I shall be your God. Let's go! [Although the Exodus required the preliminary escape from Egypt, Sinai is much more accurately to be seen as the beginning, because it was here that identity roles were established.]" "David, the progenitor of the monarchy and a man after my own heart. Let's go!" "Jeremiah, before I formed you in the womb I knew you, and before you were born I consecrated you; I appointed you a prophet to the nations. Let's go!" "Jesus, you are my beloved Son in whom I shall be well pleased. Let's go!" "Paul, apostle to the Gentiles. Let's go!" "Brethren, a people who make the New Testament their rule of faith and practice. Let's go!"

That's how, in the Bible, people find their self-identities and get launched into journeying! And psychological introspectives, still trying to get in touch with their feelings, regularly are left behind.

We have here proposed the biblical principles; let's test them against the prototype journey-launching passage of Exodus 3.

> Now Moses was keeping the flock of his father-in-law . . . and came to Horeb [Sinai], the mountain of God. And the angel of the Lord appeared to him in a flame of fire out of the midst of a bush [a place we are later told is holy ground] . . . . When the Lord saw that he turned aside to see, God called to him out of the bush, "Moses, Moses!"

And Moses, sitting there scratching on some pieces of rock (we don't have stone tablets until next time around), said, "Please! Can't I have even a moment to myself? I have spent a lifetime questing through the human pathos of slavery, oppression, flight, exile, marriage, and last but not least, sheepherding. But now—just as we were promised at Annual Conference—that journey has eventuated in a mountaintop encounter with the Divine Presence. And I would like to get it down in my journal, if you don't mind! I was trying to write: 'I have met God on the holy ground of my selfhood, experienced the numinousness of the fire that is Me in Thee. Mine is the fire—and the fire is Light, the fire is Glory, the fire is Power, the fire is Warmth, the fire is God—Me in Thee!'"

"Oh, for goodness sakes, Moses, come off it! Throw down those rocks; you will discover much more of the truth about yourself by reading *my* journal than by writing *yours.* Besides, if you'd look at the bush, you'd see that the fire already has gone out. That fire wasn't me; I am bigger than anything fire can contain. Your religious experience wasn't me; I am bigger than anything human experience can handle. You are misusing both the fire and your experience. Those were not meant to *capture* your attention — but simply to *catch* it, so that you might *pay* attention *to me*. And I'm sorry to have to tell you, but you aren't at the end of any journey. How could you be? We are only getting ready to begin. Why, I haven't yet told you who I am or what is the journey I have in mind. I haven't told you who you are or what role you are to play. I haven't even told you where we're going. So why don't you just throw those rocks away; I'll give you the tablets you need when the time is right. Get on your feet; and I'll tell you about a journey that is a journey."

> "And now, behold, the cry of the people of Israel has come to me, and I have seen the oppression with which the Egyptians oppress them. Come, I will send you to Pharaoh that you may bring forth my people, the sons of Israel, out of Egypt." But Moses said to God, "Who am I that I should go to Pharaoh and bring the sons of Israel out of Egypt?"

And Moses went on saying, "Lord, I'm sorry; but you're simply not up to date on the psychology of religion. You just can't go around telling people who *you* want them to be. Their self-identity is something they have to work out for themselves, through the trauma of the quest. And once they find the identity that feels right for them, then most people will be happy to recognize that discovery as the Divine Presence and praise you for it. But the surest way to crush a developing personality is for you to step in and try to play God. But 'leader of the Exodus'? Lord, I have kept a good journal of my faith pilgrimage and, if I may say so, am very much in touch with myself. But 'leader of the Exodus'? — that just isn't *me;* it isn't where I'm at!"

To which God replied, "I AM WHO I AM (first person); and you are going to be who I say YOU ARE (second person). So you go and tell the people of Israel that I AM has sent you and that YOU ARE going to be leader of the Exodus, whether you are in touch with such feelings or not. And, Moses, it's not polite for you always to be listening to yourself while I AM is trying to talk to you."

But Moses said to the Lord, "Oh, my Lord, I am not eloquent, either heretofore or since thou hast spoken to thy servant; but I am slow of speech and tongue." Then the Lord said to him, "Who has made man's mouth? Who makes him dumb, or deaf, or seeing, or blind? Is it not I, the Lord? Now therefore go [with God]!"

When we start preaching the psychology of religion rather than the Bible, I am afraid the Brethren wind up with Moses and need a reminder as to who created whom and who is to assign identity and role to whom. And with that, we also lose track of who alone has the right to the name "I AM" and who it is sets the journey when we go now with God.

Thus far we have examined the Annual Conference journey idea simply in the light of scripture. Yet it will be instructive to measure it in terms of "theology" (biblical theology) as well. One of the best statements of the case is probably that by Dietrich Bonhoeffer, in his famous work, *The Cost of Discipleship*. However, at this point he is building directly (and perhaps consciously) upon Søren Kierkegaard. Bonhoeffer's idea doesn't make the best sense until one knows and understands Kierkegaard.

Personally, it took me some time to get on to Kierkegaard — mainly because I didn't know the meaning of "to exist." The word of Kierkegaard's that really threw me was his statement to the effect that God does not exist, he just is. Obviously, Kierkegaard was no atheist; so how could he say that God does not exist?

The distinction turns out to be that Kierkegaard and Bonhoeffer both knew Latin and I did not. The first syllable of "exist" (the "ex-") means "out of" and "-ist" comes from the word *"sistere,"* which means "to take a position." So "to exist" is not directly synonymous with "to be"; "exists" is not identical with "is." "To exist" presupposes that the only way into existence is through an action of *becoming*. That which *is* had to get that way by *coming into existence;* it must *come* into existence in order to be. Yet not so with God, of course; he is the one and only being who just "is," who never "was not," and who never had to make the transition into existence.

Now this "transition into existence" is, of course, nothing other than what we refer to as "creation." And to this point Kierkegaard has said nothing other than that God is the Creator and that everything else is of his creation, is "creature." The best creatures can ever do is "exist"; only the Creator "is." However, Kierkegaard goes on to suggest that, when one speaks of *personal* existence, God's original act of creation doesn't entirely take care of the matter. Human beings aren't even created as full-fledged "individuals"; a further step is required in achieving personal existence, before one can exist *as a person.*

Now the term both Kierkegaard and Bonhoeffer use to identify one who has come into personal existence is "the individual" (which, we will discover, has some advantages over the contemporary fad word, "person"). But Kierkegaard in particular sees that the individual's move into existence (or perhaps, the pre-individual's move into the individuality of his existence) must involve two aspects. In the first place, he must struggle free from the undifferentiatedness of sheer mass-being — out of "the crowd" and into the particular identity of his unique individuality. But in the second place, he must also become "one" — a single, focused, centered individual in and of himself.

The word "individual," of course, means "undivided" (which is its advantage in this context). Yet, these two movements are so closely related that they may be merely two ways of saying the same thing: to exist as an individual, I must become both "one" in contradistinction to "the many," the undifferentiated mass of everyone and everything else, and "one" in the integrated individuality of my true self.

And of course, it is this quest for personhood, for personal existence, that today is the theme of philosophy, psychology, religion, and our thought-world in general. This also is precisely what the Annual Conference speakers were treating under the ideas of "journey" and "faith pilgrimage."

Very good, except: on one most fundamental point there turns out to be a polar divergency between Kierkegaard, Bonhoeffer, and the Bible on the one hand and, on the other, all secular "existentialist" thought both inside and outside the church. The secular school understands this transition into personal existence as a passionate and traumatic act of the human will, as an exercise of self-assertion, as one's creative choice of and courageous struggle for self-hood. And I could not understand the Annual Conference idea as any different from this, except in describing the achievement of selfhood as "encounter with the holy" instead of using purely secular terminology.

However, what we might call "the biblical school of theology" sees this transition in an entirely different light. The individual, now, *is chosen* for existence as a particular identity—this, rather than his *choosing* a particular identity for himself. His personal existence is as much a God-determined creation as his biological existence is. He can come out of the undifferentiated mass only because God *calls* him out into existence. And more, he has any chance of becoming truly integrated, or of becoming "one," only if he is willing to become that particular individual God intends him to be. Certainly this "becoming" requires the person's own free cooperation; but the power and direction of the move is entirely God's.

Now, as far as I know, Bonhoeffer is the first to relate this line of thought directly to discipleship. At one point (p.62), he says, "[The disciple] is called out, and has to forsake his old life in order that he may 'exist' in the strictest sense of the word. The old life is left behind and completely surrendered." At another point (p. 105) he says, "Through the call of Jesus men become individuals. . . . It is no choice of their own that makes them individuals: it is Christ who makes them individuals by calling them."

Kierkegaard had not used the idea of "discipleship" but had said almost the same thing:

> As was said in the foregoing, "the more conception of God, the more of self," so here it is true that the more conception of Christ, the more self. A self is qualitatively what its measure is. That Christ is the measure is on God's part attested as the expression for the immense reality a self possesses; for it is true for the first time in Christ that God is man's goal and measure, or measure and goal.
>
> *Sickness Unto Death,* pp. 244-45

Bonhoeffer was particularly helpful in suggesting that with which Kierkegaard certainly would agree, namely, that "disciple of

Jesus" (with the unique overtones that carries for each particular individual) is the one self-identity God intends for every person. To the extent that anyone is anything other than a disciple of Jesus, is following anything or anyone other than Jesus, he is not a true individual, either. Recall that the Great Commission specifies that disciples are to be made of all nations (or those of "every ethnic origin," as the Greek more literally says). So the thought here is at the greatest possible remove from anything in the way of self-choice, self-actualization, self-fulfillment, self-discovery, self-creation.

And the Bible's conclusion, then, goes beyond what either Kierkegaard or Bonhoeffer say in this connection. Any biblical reference to "the journey" has to do, not with one's transition into the existence of "disciple," but with the actual course of discipleship following from that. The journey is that of the now-commissioned disciple making his way through public history in the company of the brethren, following Jesus in the service of the kingdom of God.

And so the Annual Conference—the "journey" theme of which, by rights, should have had us looking to God to learn who he is; to be reminded of what identity he has assigned the Brethren and upon what journey to what destination it is he has set us; to have us considering whether we are still on the right road making right progress in the right direction—that Conference gave us little or nothing of the sort. And I felt demolished.

But Indianapolis turns out to be of a pattern with what we will find in the remainder of this study. Let me try several different ways of characterizing it:

Whether or not he was the first to come up with the idea, the renowned theologian Karl Barth was very effective in his use of the distinction between theology done "from above" and that done "from below." "From above" is invariably the biblical style. It begins by looking to God and his revelation, allowing him to define who he is; to define who we are; to tell us what is the truth about himself, ourselves, and all things; to prescribe what he would have of us. Conversely, theology "from below"—which is just as invariably *un*biblical—takes its start from our religious experience (whether the inner experience of the individual or a religio-cultural understanding of "the human condition"). Thereupon it is our religious questing that discovers (or posits) whatever of deity will best serve what we perceive as our religio-cultural needs.

Dietrich Bonhoeffer made essentially the same point Barth did — and perhaps in an even stronger way. In his Bonhoefferian study, *The Old Testament as the Book of Christ* [pp. 19-21], Martin Kuske reports it. Bonhoeffer suggests that there are two ways in which God is to be found: "Either I determine the place where I want to find God, or I let God determine the place where he wants to be found." But whoever takes the first way always finds a god "who somehow conforms to me, is pleasing, who belongs to my being." And this god invariably turns out to be what Bonhoeffer calls "a divine double, or counterpart," i.e., either as individuals or as a culture, we look into a mirror, fall in love with the reflection we see there, and call that image "God." This god, Bonhoeffer says, is also identified as being what we call "eternal truth" — with "eternal truth," of course, being "that which I already know." Accordingly, we read scripture, not at all to enable God to reveal and identify himself to us, but simply as confirmation of what our "eternal truth" already knows him to be. "Thus the interpreter claims to be able to distinguish the Word of God and the word of man in Holy Scripture. He himself [already possessing eternal truth in himself] knows where God's Word and where man's words are." Our word against God's — as it were. And this, clearly, is theology "from below."

Over against all this, then, Bonhoeffer says that the second way — namely, God's determining where he is to be found — "does not conform at all" to human preference and is "not at all pleasing." "This place is the cross of Christ." And the cross, it goes without saying, does not mark a particularly pleasant place in which to find ourselves; not a place where, as human beings, we come off looking all that good; not the place we would choose for being found out by God; not a place where we can judge God according to our eternal truth but where he judges us for our untruth. Although using different imagery, Bonhoeffer is at one with Barth in speaking of "below" and "above."

Yet, perhaps the best biblical picture of "theology from below" is the Genesis account of the Tower of Babel, that instance in which a bunch of smart people got their heads together and, rather than waiting for God to come to them, decided to build themselves up and punch through to him — perhaps the greatest religious crusade ever mounted. Unfortunately, the actual outcome of the effort was the towering babble which has marked "theology from below" to the present day — and has now provided a title for this book. What currently is new to the tragedy is the fact that such babble is heard almost as much in the church as in the world, almost as much among those who call themselves Christians as among those who oppose the faith.

As we have been hinting, it seems the case that "theology from below" has made its strongest inroads through the contemporary fashion of treating Christianity as though it were a religion. "Whatever else *could* it be?" you might well ask. And that is the crux of our problem: "religion" sounds so right to us that we can't even hear the babble involved.

Quite against my wishes, I recently got roped into teaching a college course, "Issues in Religion." We used one of the standard textbooks in the field. Slightly reworded to point up what is being said, that book's definition of "religion" reads: Religion is the human activity of attributing value to something as being pivotal for one's sense of wholeness in self and community.

I have no quarrel with that as a definition of religion and nothing better to offer in its stead. But what I wish the book would then have recognized is that none of the biblical faiths — neither Judaism, Christianity, nor Islam — come close to fitting the definition. If that is what religion is, then any biblical faith is something totally different from religion. Christianity (now to speak only of the one of those faiths that specifically concerns us) operates "from above." But, by the proposed definition, "religion" must and can operate only "from below." There is not room for, not even the possibility of, an "above" within the given definition. The "valuing" of something (to which the definition refers) is a human action that says nothing at all about whether the "something" actually does have instrinsic value — or even exists, for that matter. And of course, only the believer (and no one else) is to say whether that "valuing" does or does not give him "a sense of wholeness in self and community." Religion is not only "from below"; it is of entirely "subjective" reality.

The contrast could not be more complete. In "religion" (from below), "God" is the name we give to our inner state, "the Within" (whether that of the individual or of the human condition as such). And that "Within" is defined by the religious experience to which we attribute value. However, in "biblical faith" (from above), God is Lord, "the Without" — as defined by the biblical revelation — who can, at his own choosing and in his own way, manifest himself either through the "within" of our religious experience or through the "without" of public, historical event.

Twice in *The Cost of Discipleship,* Bonhoeffer protects biblical Christianity by differentiating it from the ancient Roman Catholic doctrine of *facere quod in se est.* That Latin phrase means "accomplishing that which is in us" and is a perfect description of the religionized distortion of Christianity so babbled among us today. In scholarly circles, in ecclesiastical circles, in lay circles, Christianity is being proclaimed as just one among the several true and beautiful world religions (and even newly invented, secular, and nontraditional "religions") by which we humans are busily "accomplishing that which is in us." It could be — it very well could be — that *religious* babble is what ultimately will bring down the tower of the church.

And as "from-below religion" does it damage, what happens is that the biblical gospel is *reduced.* We might denominate the process as "reductionism," or "reductionist theology." This style of thought does not normally proceed by openly challenging any aspect of biblical truth and denying it (by openly advocating, for example, that the New Testament can no longer serve as our rule of faith and practice). Things are much more subtle and gradual than that. Rather, the biblical witness, bit by bit, is "reduced" — by neglecting aspects of it, by changing its emphases, by interpreting it contrary to its own norms. In fact, my own hunch is that most reductionists (particularly in the Church of the Brethren) aren't even fully aware of what they are doing. They are so strongly influenced by current fashion and have such a weak grasp of biblical scholarship and theology that they have no idea but what they are proclaiming is the full-fledged biblical gospel.

Consequently, the greatest thing I could hope to have happen from this book would be for people to become so interested in their self-chosen rule of faith and practice that they become knowledgeable enough about it and skilled enough in using it that they are able to perform their own measurements and thus, for themselves, spot and call to attention any reductionism within the church. For what is certain is that, to the extent we go reductionist, we lose the name of "Brethren."

CHAPTER TWO

Getting Set Straight On Micah 6:8

For its denominational program of "Goals for the '80s," the Church of the Brethren has taken Micah 6:8 as its theme statement. However, it must be recognized that we run a real risk whenever we reduce scripture to a slogan, a logo, a banner, a catchword. The problem is that a catchword can only as much as suggest a thought which the reader must then fill out for himself. And regarding DO JUSTICE, LOVE TENDERLY, AND WALK HUMBLY, we apparently have not only run a risk but run amuck. Our mistake has been to do the filling in with our own ideas rather than with the word of God given to Micah. So let's see whether the prophet can help explain to us our own slogan—it having been anything but a slogan when Micah had it.

The book of Micah opens on a scene that is well familiar within the Hebrew prophets. God is calling the peoples of the world into his great courtroom.

> Listen, you peoples, all of you.
> Attend, earth, and everything in it.
> Yahweh is going to give evidence against you,
> the Lord, as he sets out from his sacred palace.
> For look, Yahweh sets out from his holy place,
> he comes down, he treads the heights of earth.
>
> (Micah 1:2-3 JB)

And why must there be this not particularly welcomed visit from the Judge of all the earth?

All this is because of the crime of Jacob,

the sin of the House of Israel.
What is the crime of Jacob?
Is it not Samaria?
What is the sin of the House of Judah?
Is it not Jerusalem?

(1:5 JB)

Micah lived in the time of the divided kingdom and is here identifying Samaria as the religious center of the northern kingdom and Jerusalem as the religious center of the southern. He regularly gives primary attention to his own homeland, the southern kingdom of Judah with its great temple at Jerusalem. But he here brings the surprising and most radical charge that the crime of humanity lies precisely where it considers itself at its best, namely, in its *religion*. The nation is practicing *false worship* ("from below," that is) and thus is farthest from God just where it thinks to be closest. The questioning of "worship" is Micah's major theme and the true context of our motto. We would do well to let our own worship be questioned accordingly. The worship of Micah's day was designed to fit the preferences of the worshipers, to express what would be most "meaningful" to them. Is it any different with us?

And I said:
Hear, you heads of Jacob
and rulers of the House of Israel!
Is it not for you to know justice? —
you who hate the good and love the evil.

(3:1-2a RSV)

With this, we encounter "justice," Micah's second major theme — which is not actually a second theme but simply an enlargement upon the first. What makes the nation's "worship" *false* is that it is done in ignorance or disdain of "justice." Now, contrary to much of modern thought, this is by no means to say that any and all doing of what we choose to call "justice" automatically qualifies as true worship. After all, worship certainly needs to include some knowing of *God* (and perhaps some other things) as well as knowing "justice." Nevertheless, it is made clear that there is no possibility of practicing true worship in disregard of justice.

However, Micah goes on to say that, although the leaders among his people do not know justice, he does.

> But as for me, I am filled with power,
> with the Spirit of the Lord,
> and with justice and might
> to declare to Jacob his transgression
> and to Israel his sin.
>
> (3:8 RSV)

Those words may sound very arrogant, but they are not. The prophet does not claim any special wisdom or piety that has enabled him to "know justice" as no one else does. His knowledge of justice, he tells us, has come from and with "the Spirit of the Lord" — something not at all of his own doing or for which he deserves credit. No, the coming of the Spirit happens, rather, through our openness to the Lord — which is, of course, a concomitant of true worship. Earlier we saw that "justice" must be regarded if "worship" is to be true. Here we see that it is only through true "worship" we have any chance of coming to know true "justice." As with the chicken and the egg, both of these must come "first" if we are to have either.

> Listen to this, leaders of Jacob,
> rulers of Israel,
> you who make justice hateful
> and wrest it from its straight course,
> building Zion in bloodshed
> and Jerusalem in iniquity.
> Her rulers sell justice,
> her priests give direction in return for a bribe,
> her prophets take money for their divination,
> and yet men rely on the Lord.
> "Is not the Lord among us?" they say;
> "then no disaster can befall us."
> Therefore, on your account
> Zion shall become a ploughed field,
> Jerusalem a heap of ruins,
> and the temple hill rough heath.
>
> (3:9-12 NEB)

Is the above a condemnation of false worship or of perverted justice? Obviously, the distinction cannot be made. Zion, the very place of God's house, is itself built upon the injustice of bloodshed. The first consequence of the nation's perversion of "justice" shall be the collapse of its "religious" establishment. And so the word is:

> Hear now what the Lord is saying:
> Up, state your case to the mountains;
> let the hills hear your plea.
> Hear the Lord's case, you mountains,
> you everlasting pillars that bear up the earth;
> for the Lord has a case against his people,
> and will argue it with Israel.
>
> (6:1-2 NEB)

The Judge has come to Earthtown, calling humanity before the bar of *his* justice in the Great Assize. "The Lord has a controversy with his people," as the RSV translates it. And as we will see, the motto-verse of Micah 6:8 is part and parcel of this picture. How is it, then, that we hope to get away with treating that slogan as simple ethical instruction, encouragement toward doing some things it would really be nice for us to undertake—while completely glossing over this terribly serious note of judgment? When Micah's God comes to talk about "worship," how dare we ignore the issue entirely? If God's own chosen people were this liable to charges of false worship and perverted justice, what makes us think they have no application to us at all?

It may be that, having come on so strong about the nation's *false* worship, Micah felt some obligation to talk about the nature of *true* worship. In any case, he immediately gives us an oracle on the topic—and it is to this oracle our motto forms the climax and conclusion.

> With what shall I come before the Lord,
> and bow myself before God on high?
> Shall I come before him with burnt offerings,
> with calves a year old?

Will the Lord be pleased with thousands of rams,
with ten thousands of rivers of oil?
Shall I give my first-born for my transgression,
the fruit of my body for the sin of my soul?

(6:6-7 RSV)

Micah, of course, is very familiar with Israel's priestly-cultic tradition of worship (as distinct from the prophetic-ethical tradition of worship) and here sets out to think it through and reject it. He probably knows that "the theory of sacrifice" could be given a much more favorable rationale than he gives it; but he also knows that this is the logic by which the worshipers of his day actually are operating.

If the assumption is that we please God by giving him possessions of value and that his consequent pleasure is in direct proportion to the value of that which we give, then it follows that child sacrifice would be about the most God-satisfying act one could perform. The trouble with this view, the prophet implies, is that it gives no necessary role to *justice*. More, sacrifice becomes a substitute for justice; people can continue practicing gross injustice and still claim to be in God's good graces through their ritual obedience. And ultimately, he suggests, this theory could actually lead a person into the worst sort of *injustice*, namely, the killing of one's own child.

So, not too surprisingly for a prophet, Micah rejects the priestly view of worship and opts instead for the prophetic one that centers upon ethical rather than cultic considerations.

He has showed you, O man, what is good;
and what does the Lord require of you
but to do justice, and to love kindness,
and to walk humbly with your God?

(Micah: guess what? RSV)

DO JUSTICE

It is quite possible (and I think probable) that, in presenting his trilogy—three good words defining true worship—Micah deliberately drew upon the work of a couple of his prophetic predecessors. He took the hand by throwing his trump on their two high cards, as it were—or that is how it would be in Rook, which is the only card game I know, and even that never on Sunday. But it is possible that Micah could have been personally acquainted with both Amos and Hosea, or at least familiar with their works.

However, "justice" (with "righteousness") is Amos' dominant theme. And his key oracle is constructed just as Micah's is here—or rather, Micah's is constructed over Amos' model. Amos, in his time, castigated the nation's false worship (5:21-23) and then turned to justice as the alternative. And Amos defines "justice" in a way that Micah undoubtedly also intends, although the earlier prophet managed a more accurate expression than did the later one.

> But let justice roll down like waters,
> and righteousness like an ever-flowing stream.
>
> (Amos 5:24 RSV)

The figure Amos likely envisions is that of human attitudes and behavior effectively blocking and damming up God's justice, not allowing it to flow into and through society as God would have it do. And Amos' call is for us to get out of the way and let it come. Micah also pointed to at least something of the idea when he said he is full of justice only by virtue of the fact that he has been filled with the Spirit of the Lord.

But what it comes to is that, when Micah calls us to "do justice" (i.e., when, through Micah, *God* calls us to do justice), the justice that gets done is not *our* justice nor is the doing of it *our* doing. Quite the contrary of our catchword-understanding, the call is not an ethical exhortation for us forthwith to busy ourselves in pursuing whatever our leftwing cause-groups have chosen to sponsor as the "justice" of the moment. No, for Micah, "justice" is solely the prerogative of the Lord God Almighty. And to "do justice" is simply to *let him*—let him first exercise his justice upon you, justifying *you* and making of you that which his justice requires, and then, you quit acting like a clog and start acting like a pipe, letting *his* justice roll down to float this poor world into the kingdom of God.

LOVE TENDERLY

The "tenderly" translation of our catchword marks a step *away* from Micah (as the steppers themselves now admit). Walter Brueggemann proposes that the phrase be translated to read "Love Doggedly"; and were it not for the racist overtones suggesting that only dogs and not cats are capable of loving so, this would be the step to where Micah himself stands. The Hebrew word is *hesed;* and it is the prophet Hosea who holds the copyright on this one. Here is probably his most effective use of the term:

> I [Yahweh] will make for you [Israel] a covenant on that day. . . .
> And I will betroth you to me in righteousness and in justice
> [Hosea may be preparing to play his *hesed* card on top of Amos'
> *justice*], in *steadfast love [hesed]*, and in mercy. I will betroth
> you to me in faithfulness; and you shall know [Yahweh].
>
> (Hosea 2:18a, 19-20 RSV)

Now loving *tenderly* is no big deal; we can handle that one — or at least our catchword assumes so in treating it on the same level of discourse as SAVE THE WHALES or HONK IF YOU LOVE JESUS. But practicing the *hesed* of Micah and Hosea is something else. That, if I may say so, is a doggedly of a different color. *Hesed* ("steadfast love" is the regular RSV translation) is a quality found only in God and that specifically within his covenant relationship to Israel. It is the love by which he betroths the human community to himself, as Hosea tells us. And, as *covenant* love, its first characteristic is that it hangs in and remains true even in the face of utter rejection and faithlessness from the covenant partner. Moreover, because of its very doggedness, *hesed* is the one possibility, the only possibility, for maintaining, restoring, and saving the covenant jeopardized by our human infidelity. So *hesed* is also *redeeming* love. And Yahweh's "marriage" with his people is uniquely the one that need never even contemplate the possibility of divorce, because it is cemented with the "O love that wilt not let me go."

However, the prophets never so much as suggest that *hesed* can be understood as an immediate, natural, human potentiality. Hosea does discover that he can practice *hesed* toward his faithless wife, Gomer, and thus redeem their marriage. And Micah's word does command us to exercise such doggedly redeeming love. Yet, the presupposition always is that, first, we must come to know that we are so loved *by God* and then, "Lord, make me an instrument of thy *hesed.*" Neither Micah nor Hosea could read Greek, yet they had made a memory verse of 1 John 4:19 ("We love, because he first loved us") long before John even got it into Greek.

WALK HUMBLY

To Amos' *justice* word and Hosea's *hesed* word, Micah now humbly adds his own. Walter Brueggemann—who proposed the "doggedly"—also raised the question, "On what grounds have the Brethren felt free to drop Micah's 'with God'?" Our motives, as always, undoubtedly were innocent. Sloganizing has its costs; and bumper stickers have to fit on bumpers even of the small, economy-model cars Brethren invariably drive. Yet, even the dropping of "with God" for catchword purposes would be innocent enough were it not for the fact that dropping "with God" is fast becoming a hallmark of the total Brethren theology of our day.

So let's read it Micah's way. If I suddenly were to announce that I had decided and was now going to walk (whether humbly or otherwise) with the President of the United States, the presumption involved in such an offer would be immediately apparent. Yet we can all talk about walking humbly *with God* and never see it. Nevertheless, walking with the President must depend, first of all, not upon my volunteering but upon his inviting, permitting, and making it possible. And with God, things would have to go even further. I have confidence that, if he'd let me, I could match Ronald Reagan stride for stride (after all, I am younger than he is). But walking with God? Even assuming he would let me, I am afraid his stride is somewhat longer than I am built for—which is to say that any walking with God that does occur is going to be about 99 percent *his* doing, as against my one percent willingness that it happen. And consequently, when any walking with God actually does take place, our indicated response is not the celebration of *our* walk with God but our praising *him* for the love that even wants us with him, let alone the grace that makes such companionship possible. And how presumptuous it is of us, then, to think that we are such people that our "going now with God" awaits only our own decision to do so!

Notice, finally, what happened when we let Micah reclaim the slogan he provided us. Regarding all three items — DO JUSTICE, LOVE TENDERLY, and WALK HUMBLY — we have tended to take them simply as ethical wisdom and guidance, assuming, I suppose, that we already were good enough and right enough with God that such counsel was all that was actually needed in our making the thing happen. Yet, with Micah, each of the three phrases has a much stronger reference *to God* than we have recognized.

Reference to God means "worship," and Micah presented the verse within a discussion of the nature of true worship. But we missed the cue, because, at this point in time, worshipping God as Lord isn't where we're at. Micah had set his discussion within the context of God's controversy with his people. We missed that one, too, because we can't believe God could be unhappy with folks as well-intentioned as we are. Regarding "justice," *"hesed,"* and "walking," Micah implied very clearly that it is only by going to God (i.e., worshipping) that there is any chance of our finding these. We missed that, because we have no sense of sin and thus have seen nothing to prevent us from simply proceeding with the doing, loving, and walking as the motto directs.

And then it must be said that, even as ethical guidance (which Micah's text, at least in part, is), it will be much more effective read in Micah's way than in ours — as though nothing more were involved than ethical guidance. Surely the results are better guaranteed when we are centered upon God's direct involvement rather than solely upon our own moral effort.

And all this brings us to what our entire book is about, namely, the tendency of contemporary Brethren thought — along with the whole drift of modern theology — to concentrate upon "the human condition" rather than looking to God. And this puts us precisely in place for our next chapter.

DISCIPLESHIP: antiintellectualism; anticreedalism; voluntary personal decision; inward commitment; devotional immediacy

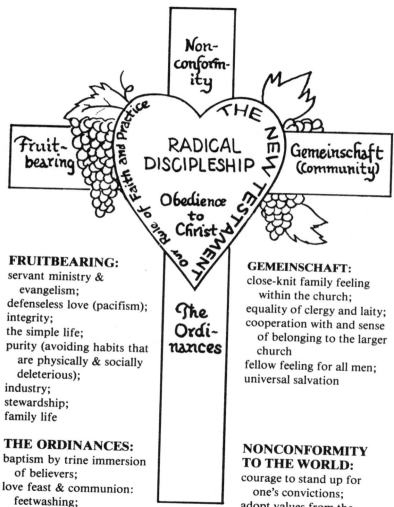

Non-conformity

THE NEW TESTAMENT our Rule of Faith and Practice

Fruit-bearing

RADICAL DISCIPLESHIP

Obedience to Christ

Gemeinschaft (community)

The Ordinances

FRUITBEARING:
servant ministry &
  evangelism;
defenseless love (pacifism);
integrity;
the simple life;
purity (avoiding habits that
  are physically & socially
  deleterious);
industry;
stewardship;
family life

GEMEINSCHAFT:
close-knit family feeling
  within the church;
equality of clergy and laity;
cooperation with and sense
  of belonging to the larger
  church
fellow feeling for all men;
universal salvation

THE ORDINANCES:
baptism by trine immersion
  of believers;
love feast & communion:
  feetwashing;
  agape meal;
  the bread and cup;
anointing for healing;
the laying on of hands

**NONCONFORMITY
TO THE WORLD:**
courage to stand up for
  one's convictions;
adopt values from the
  gospel rather than from
  society;
respect for conscience;
not afraid to be peculiar

CHAPTER THREE

The Heart Of Brethrenism

Because it is devoted specifically to an analysis of the historic tradition of Brethrenism and what is now happening to it, this will be the most particularized chapter in the book. However, the belief structure of other denominations is similar enough that, even here, I doubt whether non-Brethren readers will have any difficulty in making the application to their own churches. And I will be especially careful in explaining things for the benefit of those people.

One of my primary fields of study over the years has been the historic tradition of Brethren belief. My doctoral dissertation bore upon the subject. For a span of more than twenty-five years now I have worked at (and worked over) the chart that appears here. It has been published in several different versions in different connections. It has been accepted and used by people other than myself; no one has ever questioned its accuracy. I could support and document it at length; and I am even more certain of the chart's basic structure than I am of its details. So let's look at it.

The drawing upon which the chart is overlaid is an adaptation of a seal found upon a 1753, Germantown, Pa., deed for the first church property ever owned by Brethren. The assumption is that it is the creation of Alexander Mack, Jr., colonial leader of the church and son of the actual founder. Yet, whether that is historically verifiable or not, the design more recently has been adopted as something of a symbol of Brethrenism. The cross, of course, designates Jesus Christ and the entire Christian tradition centering in him. The heart represents the believer's heartfelt love and devotion to Jesus. And the grapes specify that such devotion is true only if it bears the fruit of lived-out discipleship.

Regarding the chart itself, it will not read correctly except by starting with the heart ("the heart of Brethrenism," of course—to justify the title of this chapter). That starting point is seen to be our deep, radical (root-driving) commitment in following Jesus as Lord and Savior. "Radical Discipleship," or "Obedience to Christ," is the way the chart has it. At the very top of the chart, then, are listed a number of implications following from this understanding of discipleship.

But back to heart itself, it is not accidental that the line "The New Testament, Our Rule of Faith and Practice" *wraps around* the discipleship commitment. It cannot be any other way. However, outside the heart, then, on each of the four arms of the cross, appear the main headings under which the specific, distinctive emphases of Brethrenism are listed. These four lists, of course, are found on either side of the foot of the cross. Present purposes do not call for us to spend time with them now; you can contemplate them at your leisure.

Let's consider, then, the chart as a whole. The secret of its arrangement is this: The crossarms represent the specific beliefs and behavior that grow out of and give content to the discipleship-commitment of the heart. Yet, the only way to get from the heart to the arms, from the commitment to its being lived out in specifics, is by studying and using the New Testament as one's rule. What does discipleship mean? Only the New Testament can tell you.

The chart deliberately does not say that the Bible represents the first and primary commitment of Brethrenism; we need to be very clear on that point. It does say that it is only through our use of the New Testament there is any possibility of fulfilling the truly first and primary commitment to follow our Lord and Savior. So if the New Testament line is left out, there is no way this chart can represent "Brethrenism." (It needs also to be noted that the line has never been understood to say "the New Testament in the absence of, or instead of, the Old Testament." It means "the New Testament *along with* the Old." Yet, it recognizes that, because the Lord we are to follow is fully revealed only in the New, that New Testament must itself also function as the rule of the Old.)

But now go back to the heart (or to the heart of the heart), if you will, and let me show you some things you missed. You missed them because they are printed in invisible ink; yet they very definitely are there. They amount to basic biblical presuppositions which lie even deeper and thus form the necessary grounding for the visible commitment to Jesus Christ as the Lord and Savior whom we are to follow in discipleship.

Scripture makes it abundantly clear that, if Jesus is to be the one to whom we totally give ourselves, we must know him, at least, as Son of God (the Word of God become flesh) and as the one whose entire mission was to proclaim, inaugurate, forward, and ultimately establish the kingdom of God. "Son of *God,*" "Kingdom of *God,*" or the biblical trinitarianism of Father, Son, and Holy Spirit—in any case, underneath the word "Christ" there *has* to be written, in letters too big to fit on the heart, G-O-D, God. He has to be seen as the thinker-upper, the creator, the motivator, the operator, the center, and the engine of this whole chart and everything on it. If GOD is not written underneath, then "Christ" and "discipleship" don't make any sense at all. If the New Testament is not "the word of *God,*" it obviously is no rule of faith and practice, either; and the whole chart falls apart.

Next comes a crucial observation: If GOD is written there in as large letters as we have suggested, then "m-a-n, man" cannot be written in that center. That center belongs to God; and God and man, Creator and creature, Potter and clay, are not so similar as to be interchangeable in that spot. Besides, if God is who the Bible says he is, then that, in itself, tells us a great deal about who man is. If God is Creator, then man is only creature. If God is Savior and Lord, then we must be those who need to be saved, on the one hand, and to be overruled, on the other. If we are to be "disciples of Jesus," then certainly we must heed his own word that "anyone who wishes to be a follower of mine must leave self behind" (not make it the heart and center of the chart). If God is in first place, then obviously man cannot be.

What may be the hardest word of scripture comes when Jesus says that even the Son can do nothing of himself (Jn. 5:19) and then tells his disciples that, apart from him, they can do nothing (15:5). Proud achievers that we are, we humans often would rather forego even the doing of great things, if it means having to admit that we can do them only with his help and by giving him the credit.

Yet, precisely here is the sticking point for many Brethren (and others) today. And the fact that they take issue with our chart on this basic a level — clear down here in the invisible ink that underlies the very heart of Brethrenism — means that, whatever they may do with anything else on the chart, they already have it skewed clean away from its original meaning. Yet, these people (as do we all) live in a society where the human self is treated as the highest value and the ultimate reality of the universe. More, this self is seen as essentially innocent and well-intentioned, the only problem being that it becomes enslaved by tradition and inhumane social structures. The goal of life, then, according to this view, is for selves to seek personal liberation and self-realization, which will then free them to join with other realized selves in building a new and liberated society.

Clearly, with this, it is now MAN (heroic, idealized man) that is writ large at the center of the chart. And where it had been written "Radical Discipleship" and "Obedience to Christ," it ought now be written "Beautiful People Diligently Using the Teachings of Jesus to Make Their Lives and the Life of Society Ever More Humane and Satisfying."

Now, for most Christians, of course, God is not absolutely eliminated from the picture, although he is given a new and different role. He is asked to vacate the center and move to one side, off the diagram, as it were — from where he is expected to contribute inspiration, encouragement, blessing, benediction, and applause for the great job humanity is doing. And so, there are Brethren pastors who, even in the administration of baptismal vows, choose to forego all such biblical terminology as sin, forgiveness, guilt, pardon, grace, redemption, repentance, or conversion — this apparently under the conviction that the human cause of getting ourselves and our world made right is not well-served by saying anything that might give people the idea that they are not good enough, smart enough, or strong enough for the job.

Although within this school of thought the Bible may still be used as a sourcebook of ideas which humanity may find helpful in improving itself, it hardly can be said that the New Testament is in any sense a "rule of faith and practice." How could it be, when its basic premises, its fundamental understandings of God and man, are being reversed, reduced, or rejected?

So notice, then, what happens to the chart and its definition of

Brethrenism when God and man thus trade places. Brethrenism now is defined by the presence of certain crossarm emphases — yet without any reference being made to the heart of the diagram, without calling attention to the fact that it has been dropped out or changed. Theological-biblical factors are treated as though they are optional and had never been an essential aspect of the faith.

(From here on out, I will make frequent use of the terms "theology" and "theological" and speak of "the Brethren aversion to theology." It is most important that my usage be clearly understood, because there are two different definitions of "theology" and thus two different "Brethren aversions to theology" which carry precisely opposite evaluations.

(In its more technical sense, "theology" identifies the effort to express the gospel by means of a highly intellectualized, rationalized, and formalized system of cognitive propositions. From their beginnings, the Brethren properly have shown an aversion to theology in this sense. The motivation was precisely the desire to be biblical — which is to say *life*-centered, as opposed to the *thought*-centered orientation of "theology."

(However, the word "theology" in itself means simply "words about God." And I want to note a modern Brethren reluctance to speak of God, even in affirming what the Bible says about him. Earlier Brethren obviously had no aversion to theology in this sense. So our two aversions are as different as this: The earlier, healthy one desisted from technical theology out of a concern to remain *biblical*. The present, unhealthy one represents a most *unbiblical* effort to de-emphasize God in the interests of playing up man. This book will now use the word "theology" only in the broad sense of words and thoughts expressive of an interest in God.)

However, at this point, my basic contention is that, once you fool around with the center of that chart, none of the crossarm emphases even mean the same thing they did when they were outgrowths of the original center. Change the roots, and you inevitably change the whole tree; the entire chart gets skewed into something completely different from historic Brethrenism.

Recently, a top leader of the denomination took a course of study at an interchurch institute of futurology, where he learned the latest methods of projecting the future of a church institution — planning for it, molding and shaping for the future deemed most desirable. Then, at the institute, he made such a study regarding the future of the Church of the Brethren. He conferred with a number of nontheologians and came up with four major emphases of Brethrenism we should give top priority in preserving—namely, peace, community, simplicity, and the fourth may have been family life (my memory fails me). All four, by the way, are items appearing on our chart.

Yet, his study nowhere gave any hint that Brethrenism even has a theological-biblical center. There was no hint that the New Testament plays any role in the church. There was no hint that the presence of God, his will for the church, and our faithfulness to that will—that these have any relevance to the future of the Church of the Brethren. No, the church was treated as though it were a totally secular organization whose future lies entirely within the scope of our shrewd planning and management.

However, my argument is that, placed within his non-theological context, even those four valid emphases identify something entirely different from what Brethrenism has always intended. The Church of the Brethren, if I may say so, is not committed to "peace." It is committed to the Prince of Peace and thus to that specific quality of not-as-the-world-gives peace which belongs uniquely to him. And those are two very different concepts of "peace." The Church of the Brethren is not committed to "community." It is committed to what Paul calls "the body of Christ" as being the one source of completely true and final community. And those are two very different concepts of "community." The Church of the Brethren is not committed to "simplicity." It is committed to seeking first the kingdom of God in such way that we let anything and everything else simply come to us as well. And those are two very different concepts of "simplicity." The Church of the Brethren is not committed to "family life." It is committed to "the Christian home," in which—both within the marriage covenant and the broader covenant that includes all the family members—God himself is recognized as one of the covenanting partners. And those are two very different concepts of "family life." If the heart of Brethrenism is neglected, changed, or reduced, no aspect of the chart any longer can be claimed as "Brethren."

In fact, contrary to the usual understanding, the items of the crossarms do *not* represent the goals and end results of Brethrenism — with the heart representing simply the "means" of their accomplishment. It is not the case that, although some people may act out of theological motives and others out of secular ones, the only important thing is that we be working for peace, social justice, community, or whatever. No, even if we were actually to achieve any of these things (whether out of faithfulness to our rule of faith and practice or, in the less likely eventuality of success, sheerly out of the resources of our own human wisdom), this would not necessarily indicate that God's will had been done and our Brethrenism accomplished its purpose.

Not hardly; because, you see, our call is not simply to do these things but to do them in a way that *witnesses* to their being the work and gift *of God*. As Jesus put it, we are so to act that people can see our good works (which is what these crossarm items are) and glorify the Father in heaven. That God be glorified is our true end; and these works of obedience are the "means" to *that* end. So our crossarm obedience, no matter how truly done, has not fulfilled its intended purpose until it points back to the heart of the chart. And that heart, we now must realize, is the end and single focus of the chart as well as its beginning and motivation.

In conclusion, then, let me treat in greater detail just one item from the chart — to show just how essential the theological-biblical center is for keeping everything else true. I have published a well-received (and even "acclaimed"?) book on the *biblical* understanding of peace and so feel I can speak with some authority on the matter. And if the New Testament is our rule of faith and practice, then the *biblical* view of peace should be the *Brethren* view, right? So let me try to put that biblical-Brethren view into a nutshell.

Perhaps the best place to start is with that favorite verse of the Brethren, "Blessed are the *peacemakers.*" We like that one — and we work hard, dedicating our best human mind and energies to "making" peace. The difficulty is that "peacemakers" is a poor translation of the New Testament Greek word standing at that point. An alternative translation would be "peace-receivers" rather than "peace-makers." Yet this would be wrong, too, because the Greek wants both of those meanings in the word, not one or the other. Actually, the text blesses only those who are "peace-*transmitters,*" those who can broadcast out only the signal that God has first fed in. It is St. Francis, again, who got the matter just exactly right:

"Lord, make *me* an instrument of *thy* peace."

However, in a more definitive way, the biblical view of peace can be summarized under four points:

(1) Scripture regularly identifies peace *(shalom)* as a prime characteristic of the final outcome of God's work with, and ultimate intention for, mankind. Therefore, to know what true peace is, where it comes from, and how it comes into being we must always look *ahead,* toward the coming kingdom of God — for this is where peace lives, this is its source and center. To pray "thy kingdom come" is the equivalent of praying "thy *shalom* be the order of the day upon earth."

Now in no way does this mean that God's peace will never be part of our experience until that kingdom is consummated at the end of history. It does mean that anything we see or know of peace in the here and now is to be understood as simply one step, one installment God has graciously granted us on the way to the real thing. Even so, any peace we know now or will ever know is not of our accomplishment but simply a God-given foretaste and preview, a still very partial (although, of course, gratefully received) anticipation of that which we can know for a fact will someday be the cosmic state of affairs.

Yet, scripture will not allow us to locate peace itself anywhere other than in this end-state kingdom of God. So just bear in mind that, in the book of Revelation, the kingdom of God is identified as "the new Jerusalem" and that the word "Jerusalem" means "City of Shalom" — it will give you a grip on the Bible's first word regarding peace.

Of course, it is necessary to remember which Jerusalem we are talking about. I heard recently that archaeologists and historians now think the Jerusalem of human construction, the Palestinian city, has thirty-seven times been destroyed by war — not too good a record as a city of peace. In addition, of course, it is the city that crucified the Son of God and over which he wept for its not knowing "the things that make for peace." Yet perhaps that is as much of a City of Peace as can be expected or hoped for from sheerly human effort. In any case, it is obvious from scripture that the true Jerusalem will have to be "the city whose builder and maker is God."

(2) In the Old Testament, then, the prophet Isaiah is the one

best presenter of this end-state vision of peace. But a most interesting observation is that his "peace" passages turn out almost invariably to be his "messianic" passages as well, the places in which he speaks of the coming Messiah. In one of these he even gives the Messiah the title "Prince of Peace," thus tying peace and the Messiah into one indivisible package. The New Testament, of course, picks up Isaiah's idea and stresses it even further. So all you need to remember, in this instance, is that the birth of Jesus was announced by angels singing, "Peace on earth," and you have a grip on our second point.

Thus far we have established that God is the inventor who started peace on its way and who will keep it going until it reaches its end and accomplishment in his kingdom. God, as it were, holds the patent and is the sole manufacturer, and he has granted the franchise to his Messiah as sole distributor.

(3) Clearly, the Apostle Paul agrees with us in understanding peace as the future, end-state reality that would come and was even now coming through Jesus. However, in the there-and-then of his own situation, the greatest peace event he could see was the reconciliation of Jews and Gentiles into the one body of Christ. Because the Jew-Gentile animosity marked the one widest, deepest, most unbridgeable conflict-chasm in his experience (and who would say there has ever been a greater?), he could propose its resolution as being the very best here-and-now preview of what ultimate, kingdom-of-God peace would be. And it is in Ephesians 2 he analyzes the ways and means of that miraculous, undreamed of Jew-Gentile peace.

He makes clear that it was not a case of some dedicated Christians taking courses in conflict resolution and then putting their skills to work in negotiating a settlement. Essentially it was the work of the God who "loved us with so much love that he was generous with his mercy . . . bringing us to life with Christ . . . raising us up with him" (vss. 4-6). God did it; but he did it through the Christ who himself *is* our peace (vs. 14). For in his own person he killed the hostility (vs. 16) by restoring peace through the cross (vss. 15-16). Thus, you who were once far off have been brought near through the shedding of Christ's blood (vs. 13) so as to create out of the two a single new humanity in himself, thereby making peace (vs. 15).

Here, then, we have added the idea that it was specifically Jesus' death and resurrection that made him not only Prince of Peace but actually the One who *is* our peace. A biblical understanding of peace has to have Jesus' death and resurrection at its center. So hang on to just one other phrase of Paul's, this from Colossians 1:20, "making peace by the blood of his cross"—and you will have our third point well in hand.

(4) Finally, although the foregoing makes it plain that peace (this kind of peace) is not something weak and sinful man would have any chance of accomplishing on his own, the biblical view does give us a real and significant role to play. It is Paul, again, who explains it, this time in 2 Corinthians 5:18-20: "From first to last this has been the work of God. He has reconciled us men to himself through Christ, and he has enlisted us in the ministry of reconciliation. . . . We come therefore as Christ's ambassadors. It is as if God were appealing to you through us: in Christ's name, we implore you, be reconciled to God [and consequently to one another]!"

In no sense, then, are we the inventors, definers, initiators, sponsors, or makers of peace. However, we are to accept it from God, cooperate with it, appropriate it into our own lives, and then witness to it, talk about it, proclaim it, and appeal to others, inviting them to accept it from God as well. We are "Christ's ambassadors"—hang onto that phrase and you have the fourth point.

Now notice what happened while we were developing this view of peace. In making the Bible the rule for the Brethren understanding of peace, in making clear that it is God's work from first to last, in seeing that it centers in Christ and that our part is to follow and speak for him—in all this we have done nothing but reiterate what our forebears already had written onto the heart of our chart—but what we have erased. So again, no item of the crossarms is accurate unless one reads it from the heart out. That way—and only that way—do we get a "Brethrenism from above."

In contrast, let's do a quick overview of current Brethren peace teaching—a reductionist "Brethrenism from below," if you will. Presently the church is talking a great deal about peace; interest may be at an all-time high. Of course, I have no way of monitoring all the pulpit and classroom words echoing throughout the congregations; but I do a rather thorough job of monitoring the printed word. It is probably safe to assume that the spoken words are generally following the same line.

Brethren peace literature comes from a number of sources. All of those now to be listed are under Brethren auspices, with greater or lesser degrees of official standing: *Brethren Peace Fellowship* has two periodical newssheets circulating in different geographical areas. *On Earth Peace* is an organization that sponsors conferences and sends occasional mailings. *Manchester College Peace Studies Institute* publishes a quarterly journal. *New Call to Peacemaking* involves the several historic peace churches but publishes literature, some of which is of Brethren origin. Our denominational magazine, *Messenger,* regularly includes peace material; and The Brethren Press produces books and curriculum pieces on the theme. Finally, there are a variety of mailings coming from the offices of the General Board, particularly the World Ministries Commission.

For anyone who tries to keep an eye on all this stuff (as I do), the first observation is that there is comparatively little that carries even hints, echoes, or overtones of the theological-biblical view we just developed. It simply isn't there. If and when there is any attempt to be biblical, it usually takes the form, "Our great teacher Jesus has called us to be peacemakers; so let's get with it" — surely a very shallow way to use the New Testament as a rule of faith and practice. Very seldom is there recognition that the Brethren peace position even has a theological-biblical base.

The impression is that such ideas are considered irrelevant to any actual accomplishment of peace. Rather, what is seen to be truly relevant is organization, propaganda, political action, social technique, schooling in international affairs and conflict resolution. In short, the heart of our Brethrenism is largely ignored. And if one were to try to deduce what presuppositions do stand written in that spot, it would probably read close to what was suggested earlier: "If You Good Brethren Would Give Your Best Thought, Skill, Time, Effort, and Money in Working for Peace, We Might Very Well Be Able to Head Off the Nuclear Arms Race and Create a Peaceful World. The Future Is in Your Hands."

Now I am all in favor of protesting the arms race and doing whatever we can in the way of peacemaking. But if this is to be the definition of Brethrenism that stands at the center of our diagram, if the accomplishment of good works by good people (mostly Brethren) is to take the place of our biblical hope of peace, then I want out. There is no evidence that this way will build anything but another Jerusalem ("City of Peace" in name only) for Jesus to weep over. There is no evidence that we—any more than those Jerusalemites—truly know what are the things that make for peace. I certainly have no intention of putting my eggs into that basket—at least not while God is standing there with his Prince-of-Peace basket into which we are invited to put all our eggs.

And so, with peace, as with any number of other items we could as well have taken from the chart, modern "Brethrenism from below"—even though claiming at least some of our historic distinctives—simply is not the real thing. It is a Brethrenism far from the heart of God—and the hymn doesn't even suggest that as "a place of quiet rest."

CHAPTER FOUR

On The Hapless Heroics of Humans

It was, in fact, from the infamous Indianapolis Annual Conference I sneaked off to a movie—only to get more of the same theology I had been hearing at the Convention Center. *Clash of the Titans* is a very religious picture. I recommend it . . . if you are interested in stupendous special effects.

Perseus is the hero of the story. He is a human being, although also a child of the god Zeus (which, of course, is how all of us are encouraged to think of ourselves these days, as progeny of the gods, seeing that to be human *is* the one true divinity). Yet, even as a boy, Perseus was the greatest, noblest, most sex-appealing thing to have come along (again, this is as we should all think of ourselves: good self image, of course).

Come to man's estate, he launches upon his heroic quest—to win the hand of the fair princess, as you might guess. Yet, in the process, he will also liberate the entire kingdom of Joppa from an evil spell (yes, it is right that heroes seek not only their own self-fulfillment but also the good of society). Perseus faces impossible odds, fights monsters, has the narrowest of squeaks, undergoes untold suffering—but brings off the final victory in great style.

It must be admitted that he does require the help of the gods (modern theology does not claim to be able to do entirely without God). However, the gods do not in any sense take over Perseus' role, win the victory, or claim credit for it. No, they only provide the means (a magic horse, sword, helmet, shield, etc.) which he can then use in his own heroic way.

The moral of the story comes in the scene where one of the goddesses on Mt. Olympus complains that, if the human race starts coming up with very many heroes like Perseus, there won't be anything left for the gods to do. To which Zeus, the father of the gods, responds that that is precisely what is supposed to happen; the gods exist to train up humanity to the place where it will not need gods any longer.

Just listen, then, and see whether today we do not get a good deal of Brethren (and non-Brethren) talk which, although done somewhat more subtly, nevertheless implies that the hope of humanity lies in our becoming the heroes we are capable of being. I once heard from a prominent Brethren pulpit an interpretation of Genesis 3 which argued that Adam's disobedience in the Garden actually marked a fall *upward,* it being essential that man break free from his dependence upon God and become the hero of history on his own. Yes, *Clash of the Titans* does present a most attractive theology. The one problem, of course, is that it is Greek paganism rather than Christianity.

However, going to our rule of faith and practice, clearly the closest counterpart to Perseus would have to be David, the boy who became Israel's greatest king and a man after God's own heart. Like Perseus, he started out, even as a youth, with all sorts of brains, bravery, talent, and glamor. Also, he, like Perseus, was favored of the gods (although, of course, just one in his case). David, too, had to fight monsters (Goliath), evade evil kings (Saul), and pull off one heroic feat after another. Yet David, too, was very successful in getting to the top spot, bringing great glory and honor upon himself, liberating Israel and making it into a more powerful nation than Perseus' Joppa ever became, and even winning the hand (and body) of the fair Bathsheba. A remarkable parallel!

Yet also a remarkable difference. At the very height of David's glory, upon his taking of Bathsheba, his story goes all to pieces. From that point until David's death — and even on into the career of Solomon and the breakup of the kingdom — everything (but everything) runs downhill. In that half of the story, there is not to be found one incident in which David comes off looking good.

So what happens? Well, scripture never quite puts it in these terms, but I think careful study would show that this is precisely what the Bible has in mind. As a result of his rise to stardom, David, understandably, got to thinking of himself as a hero, the Hero-King. And Hero-Kings, as seems only right, deserve some special privileges above those of the common people. A Hero-King, for instance, surely is not to consider himself bound to the old fuddy-duddy prohibition against adultery (as even the poorest excuse for a hero understands today).

But in the consequent decline of David, it is not that God is knocking our hero down and showing him up before the world. He doesn't have to. He is merely letting David be seen for what he really is and always has been—not a hero, but a poor, weak, sinful human being, even as you and I are. God is saying, in effect: "David, my friend, you forgot that you are a Hebrew rather than a Greek, that your story is going to be in the Bible rather than in Greek mythology, that you are dealing with Yahweh rather than Zeus. You forgot that you were not and were never intended to be the hero of this tale. In my presence, in the presence of God, for anyone to take on heroic pretensions is nothing but sin." (In fact, that wouldn't make a bad definition of *sin,* namely, the desire to be a hero before God.)

"So," God continues, "this is not a story about you, David; it is about me. And when you were looking so good, it was not because you were 'a hero' but because you were 'my obedient servant,' through whom I could and did do some wonderful things. But now that you, by claiming exemption from the commandment on adultery, have chosen to leave the servant role and pose as hero, I am going to have to withdraw my support and allow your own, self-bestowed 'heroism' show up for what it actually is."

To which David could only respond: "Lord, be merciful to me, a sinner."

———————

On this same point, I was impressed recently to discover that the present-day liturgy for Jewish Passover deliberately plays down Moses' role in the Exodus, even from what he is given in scripture. There is to be no confusion as to who is the real hero of the Exodus—and it isn't Moses.

Now, of course, Perseus- and even David-style heroism are rather obvious and blatant. Brethren, I think, are susceptible to a much more subtle and inconspicuous form of the disease. This realization hit me upon hearing a sermon that led up to and climaxed in the singing of John Greenleaf Whittier's well-known hymn—a hymn that is a favorite among the Brethren (or at least *was* until the feminist movement came along).

O brother man, fold to thy heart thy brother;
Where pity dwells, the peace of God is there;
To worship rightly is to love each other,
Each smile a hymn, each kindly deed a prayer.

For one whom Jesus loved has truly spoken,
The holier worship which He deigns to bless
Restores the lost, and binds the spirit broken,
And feeds the widow and the fatherless.

Follow with reverent steps the great example
Of Him whose holy work was "doing good";
So shall the wide earth seem our Father's temple,
Each loving life a psalm of gratitude.

Please be clear that what I am about to undertake is not particularly a critique of the theology of John Greenleaf Whittier. I have not made a broad enough study of his work to do that. I am suggesting that this one hymn is typical of a great deal of *Brethren* theology—whether it be an accurate expression of Whittier's own total theology or not. But here, once more, we find "theology from below"—this time in the interests of attributing to humans inherent qualities of moral heroism (or call it "works-righteousness," if you will).

It will turn out that our greatest Brethren strength—namely, a totally commendable emphasis on love of neighbor—is also our fatal weakness, i.e., a failure to do our works in a way that glorifies *God's* name rather than our own. A comparison of Whittier's hymn with the Gospel passage we know as the Great Commandment will show us what we need to see:

And one of them, a lawyer, asked him a question, to test him. "Teacher, which is the great commandment in the law?" And he said to him, "You shall love the Lord your God with all your heart, and with all your soul, and with all your mind. This is the great and first commandment. And a second is like it, You shall love your neighbor as yourself. On these two commandments depend all the law and the prophets."

(Matthew 22:35-40)

First and most important, Jesus makes it plain that *both* commandments are essential to the gospel. Neither dare be slighted or ignored: "On these *two* depend . . . " It is altogether right, then, that Brethrenism include a strong accent on neighbor love. Any number of the crossarm items on our chart—from peacemaking to feetwashing and beyond—can be understood as specifics under "Love your neighbor."

Nevertheless, Jesus definitely does *not* present these two commandments as being either independent from or even co-equal with each other. No, only "Love God" is called "the great and first commandment." And that "Love neighbor" is said to be "a second, like it" probably is meant to suggest that the one is actually dependent upon, or derivative from, the other. That would make good, biblical sense. In fact, even the command to love God cannot be taken as an initial, originating "first word." Biblically, it plainly is not the case that all in the world we need is the directive to love God and we then possess everything necessary to go ahead and do it. On the contrary, our loving God can happen only as a *response* to the love he has shown; to the initiative he took in revealing himself to us; to his approaching and addressing us through Jesus Christ; to his loving us, forgiving us, liberating us, and transforming us to the place where we even are capable of obeying the command to love him in return.

Likewise, it is only in our first being loved by him in this redeeming, transforming way—and then our responding with love for him—that we have any chance of discovering that the people around us are in fact "neighbors" whom we can and should love. The Johannine author makes this sequence explicit:

In this the love of God was made manifest among us, that God sent his only Son into the world, so that we might live through him. In this is love, not that we loved God but that he loved us and sent his Son to be the expiation of our sins. Beloved, if God so loved us, we also ought to love one another.

(1 John 4:9-11)

And there is not the slightest doubt that any and all of Jesus' teachings about love are to be read in just this way.

Now both the author of the hymn and its modern Brethren adherents can defend their thought as being "biblical," in that there is no denying that scripture does strongly teach love of neighbor. Yet, these proponents are grossly "unbiblical" in the reductionism of ignoring or jumping over the *sequence* by which the Bible regularly gets to this love of neighbor. The Whittier hymn starts, stays, and finishes entirely within the Second Commandment. There is here no confession, no recognition, no honoring or praising of God. At most, a nod is given to (I would prefer to say a feint made toward) the First Commandment, namely, in the suggestion that loving the neighbor *is* indeed the same thing as loving and worshipping God, *is* the worship God deigns to bless.

Of course, scripture does tell us that, *if the proper sequence is followed,* love of neighbor *can be* a form of true and proper worship, an honoring of God's name. Yet, this is not at all the same thing as saying that any sort of humanitarianism is in itself a praising of God. In such case, there would have been no need for Jesus even to have mentioned a First and Great Commandment, because doing a good job on the Second automatically would take care of it. However, even if this were true, it would still be a reversal of the biblical priority—making first what Jesus calls second, making love of God a derivation of neighbor love rather than vice versa.

Scripture, for instance, in effect says that wherever God has extended his "peace"—in the way of forgiving people, redeeming them, transforming them, making Christians of them—*there* you are certain to find "pity" (neighbor love) dwelling. But to turn things around to say that, wherever you find human pity dwelling, that is the equivalent of God's being present in his peace—that is quite another idea and one coming perilously close to putting God under our control and making him a creature of human piety.

It is rather apparent that the wide divergence of thought between Whittier and Jesus ultimately roots in a difference of *anthropology,* that is, differing evaluations of what is the moral status and natural potential of human beings. That the Bible finds it essential to specify the gracious work of God as prerequisite to our loving of the neighbor clearly implies that human beings, as they are, simply do not have the wherewithal to bear the fruits that God would have of them. Our sin and weakness constitute a blockage with which God, on his own, will have to cope before there is any possibility that true neighbor-loving can take place. Indeed, scripture indicates that our problem is such that, even when neighbor-loving does get practiced, it is to be understood as God's channeling *his* love through us, rather than its being the implicit lovingness of our dispositions finding a natural outlet.

Nevertheless, we *do* see and feel neighbor-loving taking place. And according to the biblical understanding, when that does happen we have no alternative but to praise God for that which never in the world could have happened apart from his presence and power.

Yet, the view represented by the hymn is the complete opposite of this. Here we proceed directly to the Second Commandment, because no prerequisites are considered, no blockage is sensed, no problems envisioned. All that is necessary in getting neighbors loved is that natural-born lovers (Hero-Lovers, if you will) be inspired to do it. And the hymn, note well, consequently reduces God's role to that of Great Example who shows and tells us the best way to do our neighbor-loving and that of Blesser who then congratulates us for doing it. In any case, the fact of the matter is that Whittier's hymn does neither praise nor credit God in any significant way.

We have proposed that the initial divergency here lies in whether human nature does or does not include a problem of *sin* which makes God's gracious work of redemption absolutely essential to true piety and the success of the human venture. However, the end consequence of that divergency becomes polar separation. Scripture as a whole—beginning either with Jesus' Great and First Commandment or the Old Testament *Shema* (the "Hear, O Israel" of Deuteronomy 6:4-5)—is fundamentally GOD-centered, leaving us absolutely no option except to praise God from whom *all* blessings flow. Yet, the line of thought represented by Whittier's pean to neighbor love leads quite otherwise. It is fundamentally MAN-centered, celebrating human nobility and our potential for greatness. Sermon, song, and litany now are designed to inspire us to the exercise of such moral heroism, assuring us that we will win God's blessing in the effort. The First Commandment and the praise of God are definitely muted. And why? Because if *we* are the ones who do this neighbor-loving, what is there to praise him for? It isn't as though he were Lord and Savior or anything of that sort.

Let me get bring this point somewhat closer home by examining a second hymn—one of contemporary Brethren rather than ancient Quaker origin. (I should say that, musically and poetically, I like this hymn very much; it is only *theologically* I find it weak.)

REFRAIN:
For we are
Strangers no more, but members of one family;
Strangers no more, but part of one humanity;
Strangers no more, we're neighbors to each other now;
Strangers no more, we're sisters and we're brothers now.

Come walk with me; we'll praise the Lord together,
As we join song to song and prayer to prayer.
Come, take my hand; and we will work together
By lifting all the burdens we can share.

REFRAIN:

Where diff'ring cultures meet we'll serve together.
Where hatred rages we will strive for peace.
Come take my hand; and we will pray together
That justice come and strife and warfare cease.

REFRAIN:

There is a love that binds the world together;
A love that seeks the last, the lost, the least.
One day that love will bring us all together
In Christ from south and north, from west and east.

REFRAIN:

As with Whittier's, this hymn has a point of contact that would seem to make it quite biblical. In this case, the passage is Ephesians 2:4-22 (NEB)—which we touched upon in the previous chapter:

You who once were far off have been brought near. . . . Gentiles and Jews, he has made the two one, and . . . has broken down the enmity which stood like a dividing wall between them . . . so as to create out of the two a single new humanity . . . , thereby bringing peace. [And the RSV concludes:] You are no longer strangers and sojourners.

Obviously, I here have edited Paul very heavily in order to make his text and the hymn as congruent as possible. Yet my best effort couldn't quite bring it off. Paul insists on speaking of "he who has *made us* strangers no more," rather than simply of the fact that we *are* strangers no more. Let me go back and give you a truer edition of what Paul had to say:

> But God, rich in mercy, for the great love he bore us, brought us to life with Christ even when we were dead in our sins. . . . It is not your own doing. It is God's gift, not a reward for work done. . . . But now *in union with Christ Jesus* you who once were far off have been brought near *through the shedding of Christ's blood* . . . so as to create out of the two a single new humanity *in himself,* thereby making peace. [Back to the RSV:] *So then* you are no longer strangers and sojourners.

The root distinction between the scripture and the hymn is actually signalled in their opening phrases: where Paul says, "But *God,* rich in mercy . . . ," the hymn says, "For *we* are . . . ." Yes, it is true that the hymn (as with Whittier's) has some references, such as "we'll praise the Lord," "we will pray," "there is a love," and "in Christ," which at least hint that we are talking of more than sheerly human process. However, these certainly are neither specific nor emphatic enough to constitute a focus the equivalent of Paul's.

The hymn, clearly, is intent upon celebrating the fact that we are indeed strangers no more. But before Paul can get to that point, honesty impels him to recount God's gracious work and praise him for bringing us to the place that we *can* be strangers no more. And what a work that was! Because we were "dead in our sins," he had to "bring us to life with Christ" before there could be any thought of reconciling us to himself and to one another in him. And even then, the "dividing wall" of our enmity was such that it took "the shedding of Christ's blood" to bring it down. Before Paul could talk about our being strangers no more, he had to talk about the love of God that redeems us from sin, about God's becoming incarnate in Christ, about Jesus' atoning death and victorious resurrec-

tion, about our coming to be in union with him—a real mouthful of
theology ("words about God," and all of them "from above").

And when the hymn (as with many contemporary Brethren
and other Christians) wants to speak of our being strangers no
more, yet without getting involved in a lot of "theology," the impression definitely is left that the creation of the strangerless community actually requires only our readiness to extend the invitation,
"Come, walk with me and take my hand." At least the hymn
recognizes no hindrance that would call for a special act of God,
nor does it give us any particular cause to praise or credit him. And
so must it be with any reductionist treatment of the gospel that
prefers to avoid theology.

Now surely it must be recognized that both of these hymns
have in mind an "ethical intention"; they want to inspire us to the
actual practice of neighbor love in the one case and to truly
demonstrating that we are strangers no more in the other.
However, it must be said that the respective scripture passages are
just as ethically interested as are the hymns. Jesus' two commandments and Paul's proclamation of strangerlessness are in the New
Testament to no other purpose. So the only question is, which approach should prove more ethically effective, the biblical or the
hymnic?

The hymns—in presupposing that, by nature, we already are
equipped to love neighbors and live strangerlessly—they need only
and *can* only exhort: "We can do it; we really can; so let's go out
now and do do it!" However, the scriptures—in praising God for
what he has already accomplished for us and in us—certainly compel us to confess that he has not only commanded what we should
do but has made us capable of doing it and has actually offered to
do it through us if we will but let him. In the biblical approach, the
ethical fruit is as much as guaranteed by God. Yet, quite the contrary, the approach of the hymns leaves the matter entirely dependent upon the frailty of human piety, power, intelligence, and
motivation. So Christian ethics is not something different from
theology; it is theology doing its proper work.

(I trust it is evident that my purpose here has not been to make
a target of two particular hymns or their authors. My concern is
with the much broader phenomenon of Brethren aversion to
theology. The hymns have served simply as examples for dis-

cussion—and there are any number of other hymns that would have served as well. And even regarding the hymns themselves, my personal conclusion may be found surprising: These two hymns—and others like them—can be appropriate and useful, *if* they are put within a setting of sermon, litany, scripture reading, and other hymns that, in effect, corrects their deficiency and fills them out. Thus the service in its entirety can come to focus as a truly biblical faith statement in a way the hymn by itself cannot. It is only when whole services fail to rise above the level of these hymns that there is matter for concern.)

Notice, finally, that this long discussion can be put very briefly in terms of the Brethrenism chart of the previous chapter. The hymns represent just one more attempt to go directly to the crossarm distinctives (neighbor love, community, or whatever), define Brethrenism in terms of these, and effectually deny that our tradition even has a theological-biblical center.

My studies indicate that this sort of heroic anthropology and human-centered faith—although in comparatively mild form—first entered Brethrenism under the aegis of the Social Gospel during the second quarter of this century. (An interesting exercise is to leaf through the *Brethren Hymnal* classifying those hymns that are predominantly God-centered as against those predominantly man-centered. It will turn out that very few of the older hymns fall into the man-centered category and that virtually all that do will have been written during the Social Gospel period and since.) In the current fourth quarter of the century, then, the earlier tendency has intensified through the influences of what Christopher Lasch calls our "narcissistic [read: self-centered] culture."

It is my impression that, back there in the period of the Social Gospel, the Brethren jumping-of-the-track happened in this wise: The church took the position that (1) we want to emphasize what is most central and important in the New Testament and be less concerned and relatively free regarding things that are not so important. Therefore, (2) we will be very strict on Jesus' ethical teachings but quite lax on "theology" (beliefs concerning the nature and activity of the Godhead).

Now it seems plain that Statement #1 is entirely correct. There is no other way of using the New Testament as a rule of faith and practice except by reduplicating its own emphases. But from where came the idea that Statement #2 is an accurate application of Statement #1? There is no way an objective, open-minded examination of scripture can be made to support "ethics, yes; but theology, no." The fact of the matter is that Brethren did not use the New Testament rule to let it tell them how the New Testament itself is orchestrated. They took on a humanistic bias from the world and fashioned for themselves spectacles which gave them a completely distorted reading of the gospel.

I am not implying that it would have been truer to have reversed the priorities to "theology, yes; but ethics, no." That would have been just as wrong. The fundamental error came, rather, in posing a distinction between theology and ethics that even allows a difference of priority or emphasis. Every bit of Bible study undertaken in this book points to the conclusion that biblical theology is the source of biblical ethics, just as biblical ethics is the necessary outcome of biblical theology. You can no more emphasize one over the other than you can expect an answer to the question, "Which is more important to a spoon, the handle or the bowl?" Obviously, until you have both (and properly connected, it must be said) you don't even have a spoon. Yet it is precisely because they lost the essentiality of "bowl plus handle *equals* spoon" that the Brethren have now wound up with, for example, a peace emphasis which, lacking any solid theological grounding, can't be anything close to "the biblical peace ethic."

Now for some denominations, this theologically anemic "ethical humanism" may have been the price that had to be paid in getting social concern and neighbor love built into their Christian understanding: But that need never have been the case with the Brethren. Our chart portrays Brethrenism as it has been from its 18th century beginnings and thus is living proof that true social concern *can* proceed out of a handle-*and*-bowl, biblically-oriented, God-centered, theologically-sound heart and core. Regarding both the second quarter Social Gospel and fourth quarter Narcissism, then, we should have been using our Brethrenism to correct *them* rather than letting them "correct" our Brethrenism. But, sorry to say, we have not done a very good job of resisting the influences of the world and have jeopardized our Brethrenism in the process.

Above all, at the heart of our faith, we dare not allow the

glorifying of the human to encroach upon our glorifying of God. And to this end, I now propose a minimum, core theology consisting of eight points which I consider to be absolutely essential:

CORE PRINCIPLES OF A BIBLICAL THEOLOGY

(1) *God is Lord and Savior, his one objective being to bring all things under his own kingly rule.* The coming of God's kingdom is the focal goal of everything that is and happens; and as the Lord's Prayer has it, "thy kingdom come" means nothing other than "thy will be done on earth."

(2) *The kingdom being entirely his own concept, plan, and accomplishment, God alone is worthy of all honor, glory, and praise.* (See Chapter Six.)

(3) *We are called to serve his kingdom rather than his serving whatever we see to be our needs or whatever goals we set for ourselves.*

(4) *Our own needs will best be met by letting God do things his way.* We do not mean to say that God has no concern about human needs. Yet, rather than focusing upon what we conceive as our needs, bending all our efforts and enlisting God to get them cared for, we are to concentrate on serving him. In the process, we will discover that our own needs have been cared for in a better way than we could have foreseen. "Whoever will lose his life for my sake will find it."

(5) *Human ego-assertiveness, any desire to look heroic in the sight of God, is sin.* In light of the Genesis 3 account of the Fall, this would even stand as a rather good definition of sin.

(6) *Man does indeed have true greatness when he is willing to accept it from God rather than claim it on his own.* Properly understood, the Bible consistently supports the glory of our being human rather than denying or belittling it.

(7) *God the Father has put the coming of his kingdom entirely into the hands of Jesus Christ, making him its sole administrator and agent.* Jesus proclaimed the coming of the kingdom, made it present through his own obedient ministry, won its victory through his death and resurrection, as living Lord is now furthering it through the Spirit's activity in the church and world, and will bring it to consummation in his coming again.

(8) *More specifically, Jesus' atoning death and victorious resurrection constitute the pivot and key of this entire work of God.* The New Testament makes clear that the gospel can focus nowhere else.

Of course, no claim is made that these eight points make up a full-fledged Christian theology. There are major areas of doctrine that aren't even touched. Yet, I suggest that just this much would have us positioned right for hearing and understanding the rest. On the other hand, if we are outside any of these parameters, anything we read in scripture is bound to become skewed and distorted.

I have a friend who, any time I mention the New Testament as a rule of faith and practice, objects that that is to say nothing at all, because, by fine-tooth-combing the Bible, you can find support for anything you want to believe. Now that may be at least partially true regarding some minor points upon which you have to look hard even to find scriptures that apply. Yet, regarding each of our eight points, any honest biblical scholar — or even casual student — would have to agree that these are basic premises assumed at virtually every point of scripture. They are concepts which could be documented almost by opening the Bible at random. This core, I would argue, is "biblical" in a much more profound sense than simply saying that, if we had to, we could find a verse somewhere supporting the idea.

Yet, my opinion is that, by and large, this bedrock biblical theology is not what we hear coming through the greater part of our Brethren literature or from most of our pulpits (as it is not being heard in many other churches either). As the voice of our rule of faith and practice, this *should* be pre-eminently the Brethren theology. But since we are not getting much of it from the Brethren, could I recommend where we might find it?

I could; and though I will be accused of book-peddling, I am going to proceed anyhow. J.C. Blumhardt and his son Christoph were a team whose successive pastoral careers in southwest Germany spanned from the 1840s to about 1920. In addition to being more Brethren than the Brethren (although they were actually renegade, kicked-out members of the Reformed Church), their theology has the advantage of consisting not in egghead books and university-level lectures but in informal talks and sermons delivered to the laity.

After years of collecting, selecting, and translating their material out of the German, in 1980 I published a volume of Blumhardt quotes and excerpts entitled *Thy Kingdom Come*. What follows are a few pieces out of that book. As you read, I invite you to judge (1) whether the Blumhardts do not beautifully present and emphasize our eight points, (2) whether what they say does not ring very true to what you know of the Bible, and (3) whether — at least to Brethren ears — this does not sound right as to what Brethrenism truly is and ought to be.

THE ALL-ENCOMPASSING REALITY OF THE KINGDOM

There must be a new reality which is of the truth. It is not to be a new doctrine or law, not a new arrangement. The new truth to which we must listen is that which came in the person of the Son of Man himself, namely, that God is now creating a new reality on earth, a reality to come first among men but finally over all creation, so that the earth and the heavens are renewed. God is creating something new. A new history is starting. A new world is coming to earth.

The earth shall be filled with the glory of God. According to the Bible, that is the meaning of all the promises. Jesus, come in the flesh, what is his will? Of course, nothing other than the honor of his Father on earth. In his own person, through his advent, he put a seed *into the earth.* He would be the light of men; and those who were his he called "the light of the world" and "the salt of the earth." His purpose is the raising up of the earth and the generations of man out of the curse of sin and death toward the revelation of eternal life and glory.

Truly, within the human structures of sin, we have no lasting home; we must seek what is coming. But what is it, then, that is coming? The revealing of an earth cleansed of sin and death. This is the homeland we seek. There is no other to be sought, because we do not have, and there cannot come to be, anything other than what God intended for us in the creation.

Lo, I am with you always, to the close of the age. (Matt. 28:20)

The Savior's being with us has reference to the end of the world, not to its continuance. All the days of the disciples of Jesus are work-days looking forward to the consummation of the kingdom of God, with which event the present futile world will come to an end.

In the special sense of our text, Jesus is not *with* a person who spends his days for the sole purpose of sustaining earthly life. The Lord does not wish to spend too much effort on the continuance of the world. After all, it is corruptible; there is nothing left to be done but to await the wearing out of the decaying structure and the creating of a new one.

In all our work, then, let us be careful to fix our eyes, not on the continuance of the world, but on its end. Then the Lord will be with us always, and he will see us through our current needs as well.

THE SIGNIFICANCE OF JESUS

When Jesus came into our company, it was day. . . .
The whole history of humanity pivots, one might say, upon the works of Jesus, All that has come to pass since—the good and the evil, the bright and the dark—everything turns upon these works of Jesus which are directed toward the future of humanity.

Jesus, who is the glory of God on earth, wants to help us become the same thing. In this man, God again shines forth. It is for a purpose, then, that he is here; he acts as God in the creation, among men. This is his work; consequently, he has eternal life and does not perish even though nailed upon the cross. Nothing, no possible situation, even the most disadvantageous you could conceive, can overcome this man, because he is here to accomplish something.

From him shines forth the Father of creation. And the creation feels that once more it has been given hope, as it were, because this man understands what needs to be done so that the things of God might again be brought into order and the ruined, wasted earth again be restored to him. I tell you, such is the Savior's first order of busi-ness. The Savior is, first of all, "for" God and only then "for" you. Bit by bit, man has turned things around and made the case appear as though the Savior had come only *for us*. Thus people use Jesus to flat-ter themselves; but this eventually can bring things to a pretty pass. I tell you, therefore, the Savior doesn't care about *us*, he doesn't even care about people as a whole—if they will not help *him*.

THE SOON-COMING OF JESUS

The Lord Jesus is the beginning and the end regarding the kingdom of God. Therefore, among us, it firmly and with certainty is said, "The Savior is coming again!" He must complete the work; and we have only to be his servants until he comes again. As servants, we must serve him, the Coming One.

At the same time, we should be a prefiguring of the future of Jesus Christ on earth. We should not be so much concerned with ourselves; nor should we struggle so hard, as though we were the ones to bring the good to its perfection on earth. We cannot do that. That can be done only by the Lord Jesus, who has come the first time and is coming again a second time.

He will complete the work; we will not. We must lock this knowledge in our hearts; it must be true and firm whenever we preach the gospel. Our way must always be lighted by this star, "He is coming again!" And if our minds are directed toward the coming of the Savior, this puts the entire gospel into its true perspective. The gospel will become something personal and living when we firmly and faithfully focus upon the words, "He is indeed coming again!" When we fail to do that, then we are separating the gospel from his person. Then, no matter how much we talk or what great speeches we make about it, we are nevertheless separating him from the gospel. Without his personal presence, not a word of the gospel has real or profound value.

And so we must be directed toward that future coming of Jesus Christ which is not only something of the future but also of the present, in that he right now is awaited in our hearts. . . .

We are living in a time of death; and we don't want to hide that from ourselves. Our powers become weak; our ideas lose their strength, and our feelings do also. Even though they be alive for the moment, with time they are lost. The law of death surrounds everything, all we do and think and feel. But now a law of life comes into this world of death. It is actually the Lord Jesus himself, the one who is eternal life, who is arisen from the dead, who links us to the other world, who brings us the Spirit of God that, in the midst of our dying life, again and again we might receive something fresh and living through his gift, through his presence, through his coming.

We are not to think of his coming only as an appearance at the end of days. Rather, we must at all times have an awareness of the coming Savior. Each of us should continually have that in mind, even in times of darkness, in times of depression, in times of poverty, in times of sickness, in times of trouble, and in times of work with the things of earth.

TRUE MAN

He is the glory of God upon earth and the glory of man in heaven. Just as God was blotted out on earth, so also was man blotted out in heaven. Now Jesus comes as the one he is; and God lives upon earth. Then Jesus is again with the Father in heaven; and humanity lives there in him. Now before God there gleams something of the humanity which was dead; it is the glory of mankind in heaven before God through Jesus.

Mark this well: The kingdom of God takes shape through nothing other than the coming of the Lord. It is not formed through any human discovery, no matter how worthy and honorable. . . . Yet it is remarkable that, for all of this, not only God, the creator of the heavens, but also *men* must be in on the plan. But this makes sense. For if there were no people at all involved, but only God, then truly it would have to be said that man was *not* created in the image of God. Nevertheless, man *shall* be in the image of God and shall remain so; as such, he shall become the co-worker of God in the most great and most holy work of that which God purposes for his creation.

True man is missing. . . . *False men with a false spirit, with false* desires and false aims, think that they are real men. . . . The false man is the world's undoing. . . . True man is still missing and will be missing until Jesus comes and does away with the false man. . . .

Yet now we do have the fortune to know that there is one in whom the world is God's again, in whom all that is created is again placed into the light of the first creation. This one is Jesus. . . . Jesus, the Son of Man, is more real than any other man, more childlike than all other children. He lives among men, and he is the kingdom of God. He does not *make* it; he *is* the kingdom! Why? Because he is God and man.

When God created the world he founded his kingdom on earth. The earth was his kingdom. And who was to reign, to rule, and to watch over it as his representative? *Man*. God's kingdom was in paradise through man. God's kingdom is on earth through one upright man, no matter what men are like otherwise. . . . One true man—and God's kingdom is here! . . . An Adam, and there it was, God himself in paradise. Even if here and there something wrong was still lurking in corners, that didn't matter. A man was there, and God was with this man. Nothing else was of any importance. . . .

The loss of man was the world's catastrophe. Man was gone. This is still the world's undoing today. . . .

Now Jesus seeks a *living church*, and he seeks it on earth. Could not the one who rose from the dead have come quickly, in heavenly glory, to conquer and overcome all things? He would have done it long ago, without hesitating, if this would have made God's kingdom possible. He could have come with hosts of angels. But no! He doesn't want only angels. Man, not super-worldly powers, must serve God on earth. True man must do it; and God must do it in him. This is Jesus' loyalty toward us false men.

HUMAN HUMILITY

And man, in the midst of creation, has the feeling that he is here for a purpose—not just for himself but for something else, something greater, something which has been lost.

Nevertheless, today people sit in the churches thinking mostly about *themselves!* Everyone sighs over himself, looks for something in himself and for himself—and doesn't himself know what it is. One would like to call out to them all: "People, forget *yourselves!* Think of *God's cause.* Start to do something for *it.* Don't be sorry for yourself; or at least be sorry that you have nothing to do but worry about your own petty concerns."

Our greatest lack is that we are of no use to the Lord; no wonder, then, that we go to ruin in spite of all our culture. Any person degenerates, even in a physical sense, if he is not acting as part of a body that has a higher purpose. But those who, in love and enthusiasm, work for something greater than themselves prosper, even regarding their physical well-being. And the race declines in its very life-values, both physical and spiritual, if, as people, there is nothing we are producing for the life of the earth, for creation, for God.

Leave for a while your begging before God and seek first the way, the way in which we truly can know God, by recognizing our guilt and in truth seeking only the righteousness of God in his rule upon earth. Put aside your own suffering and start doing honest works of repentance, doing them with joy, not with sighing and complaining, giving God the glory in body and soul. Then accept your guilt and its judgment and become a true person. Thus, through Christ, you will be bound to God; and your own suffering and need will fade of itself.

Turn about in the inward man and, instead of looking at yourself and all your need, look to the kingdom of God and its need; it has been held back for so long because of the false nature of man. Then you can be confident that God will treat you as a true child who is seeking *his* honor, and you will not come to shame in this life.

I have for all of you a heartfelt concern before God; and I so much want to help. However, I know of nothing to say but, "Remain firm, firm in doing what God wants." The kingdom of God must be the desire of our hearts; then solutions will come. You can be useful when you are willing to bear the greatest misery for God's sake. Even in a bodily sense you will not go under, whether or not that seems to be the case. It cannot be in vain, bearing what God wills us to bear, when we are following the one who bore the cross.

DIE, AND JESUS WILL LIVE

We observe Christendom deteriorating and becoming bound up in the temporal. . . .

All we have had up to this point is on its last run downwards. Our theology is moving down with the rapidity of a lowering storm. Our ecclesiastical perceptions are rapidly becoming political perceptions. Our worship services are being accommodated to the world. And thus it is necessary that all that has been should cease, should come to its end, making room again for something new, namely, the kingdom of God.

And we have a certain right to expect this in our time. At least I would like to stand before you as a witness of the truth that we are living in a day when we can expect the end of that which has been and can hope for the new. . . . Together with those who belong to me and all those who wish to understand me, my one aim shall be to permit that which has been to die, to cease. Of course, this is to take place in spirit, not outwardly. God wants to introduce some new thing; and the Savior will be better able to live in us when we ourselves no longer want to amount to so much—when we acknowledge that in what has been until now there is much that is detrimental, much that is of the flesh, much *human* activity, although the intentions were good.

All of this must die; therefore, we now say: "Die, then *Jesus* will live."

It is more important that the Savior overcome *us* than that he continue to attack the devil. The devil is not so significant; we ourselves are much more truly the opposition to the kingdom of God. We who are in the flesh offer much more resistance to the kingdom of God than the devil does. Human self-will, earthly-mindedness, and greed; the will to power and the love of fame; human heroism which does not need God but in the strength of youth accomplishes what it chooses without consulting God—these overleap the commandments of God and prove more dangerous than the devil. If in our day we wish to fight as we ought, then we must turn against these foes.

You will understand, of course, that in this conflict one does not advance *heroically,* as one does in fighting the devil. Here one becomes weak. And here I need to become the weakest among you. Only in dying do I want to become the strongest among you—in self accusation, in gladly taking the guilt of others upon myself, in willingly suffering in myself all the pain and the cares of others. In this, I want to be the strongest among you. But, beloved, I do not wish to do it alone. . . . Follow me into this much more difficult struggle in which we turn the sword upon ourselves. . . . We want to be those who are dying, because we know that very soon we must give account to the Lord for everything we have done. . . .

RESURRECTION

If I must give up hope for any person in any respect, then Jesus is not risen. I tell you this before God and his angels, before Jesus himself,

"You are not the light of the world if I have to give up hope." . . . For me, this *is* the resurrection of Jesus Christ.

This is the great triumph of the resurrection of Christ: people are born, people who already live. But those who live in sin and death are born again; and in them something new is revealed through the tremendous power of Christ Jesus. . . .

I ask you, "Friends, from where does humanity draw its life? From where does Christianity draw its life?" We can answer with certainty: From those in whom the resurrection of Christ has repeated itself, those of whom it truly is said, "He who believes in me, though he die, yet shall he live, and whoever lives and believes in me shall never die" (John 11:25-26).

It is through *these* people that the world endures even today. In them lives Jesus, the one risen from the dead. In them he rules and in them is victor. In them he is grace, is the light of the world. In them he will be glorified through all creation.

JUDGMENT

God's ways lead through judgment; and that judgment must create good. A cleansing shall take place in our unclean society; and the word of God shall remain our light and comfort even in the death of an age and its culture. The kingdom of God will now be prepared in earnest; and I rejoice that, in his earnestness, God is now speaking with mankind. This is itself a grace which remains firm in our hearts. Trouble and the works of men will pass away. God's grace and the victory over sin, death, and hell will become fact even in our time.

Now is the time to take upon ourselves a work in which we are the first to be given into judgment, not the first to have a sofa in heaven. For only those who are truly first, first to stand before the Savior in judgment, can become tools to further his work among the rest of mankind.

What I see as the greatest danger for most people is that of judging themselves and others against a norm set up by society, one by which people can flatter themselves. And this self-justification becomes a powerful force. As a stance before God, it is colossal autonomy. In that situation, one dare not raise any questions about the encompassing social milieu.

Ultimately, however, the *only* thing of importance is God's opinion. Men can neither justify nor damn; only God can. . . . To be able to live *before him*—this is what we must seek. We don't need the slightest recognition from men; and we don't want it, either. We need only God's recognition on earth. His freedom, nobility, and superiority must captivate us. I do not want to be dependent upon anything else, so that I can be completely dependent upon God, his eternity, truth, and greatness.

The greatest goodheartedness and kindness in a populace, even the best of wills, is of no advantage regarding that for which Jesus came. He came to raise mankind completely out of earthly things and into the heights of God. And in doing that, he first of all forces earthly things *out* of the heights of God. And no society is about to let that happen.

So it has been, even to the present day. One can, in a manner of speaking, *enculturate* Christianity and even bring it to power; but then it is no longer what Jesus had in mind. Even such "Christian" powers —which ultimately are in opposition to the Spirit of God—will be displaced by other powers or else become bound up with them; and the whole world will again be running on the same old tracks. There is no track driving through to Christianity.

THE LITTLE FLOCK

God makes use of us. We must not want to make use of Jesus for our- selves but must want Jesus to make use of us, must want to give ourselves entirely to his use.

Meanwhile, God does not need much upon earth. He needs only a few yet *total* persons; he can lay hold of these few, so to say, and by them the whole world can be held firm. Do not consider yourselves too insignificant, dear friends. Leave behind the ordinary disposition of people who think that there must always be large masses representing the kingdom of God on earth. It is much better when we are a little band.

One, two, three, ten people who are united are stronger than a hundred thousand who thrash about in their piety yet never arrive at a true and unanimous striving for the kingdom of God.

Until Jesus comes, his will remain a "little flock." Yet this is not simply because only a little flock are to be called to glory—oh, what an awful mistake! no! no!—it is because the rest of the poor people simply have not the wherewithal to bring off the assignment. . . . But the little flock arrives at the goal; and it is through this flock that the kingdom will be given. . . .

*Our dear God never lets his little flock become prominent. They are al-*ways in the background. They might be ever so successful and strong within themselves; but they will never win human fame through human deeds, not even if they be the finest of prophets or angels. Indeed, precisely because they are such, they must remain hidden. Our dear God is not about to strike a deal with mankind on the basis of any great personages he can claim for himself. . . .

When we look back over the history of mankind, we see a forest where trees once grew but where the storms have passed, laying it waste. In this, in the whole unhappy course of mankind, our dear God is still the manager who allows people—who must belong to *him*—to be his saints. These are people in whom he is a power and to whom he simply says, "You must go my way and demonstrate that, even under evil conditions, a way is to be found which can be traveled without becoming entangled." . . . Always, when things are to move forward, God must have saints who also stand in their own times; who understand the times; who know how to live among the people of the times; but who, even though the times be ever so perverted, still carry the high thoughts of the kingdom of God in their spirits.

CHAPTER FIVE

On Selective Sin and Righteousness

Two chapters back we were talking about the Brethren peace position. In the chapter immediately preceding we focused upon human heroics. We now bring those themes together with another style of human heroics, using our peace position as a specific example. The insight came to me out of a study by a professor of New Testament from the University of Tuebingen (Germany), Martin Hengel. I might as well tell the whole story.

Hengel has specialized on the first-century Jewish revolution against the Roman military establishment, the proponents of which came to be known as the Zealots. The spirit they represent ("zealotism," we shall call it) marks, I think, a great deal of modern thought both in the Church of the Brethren and other churches. So in the following, a capital-Z "Zealotism" designates the first-century phenomenon and lowercase-z "zealotism" the timeless manifestation of it. And zealotism—I want to show—is precisely "selective sin and righteousness."

Hengel has two, slim (almost booklet) volumes, *Was Jesus a Revolutionist?* and *Victory Over Violence* [both from Fortress Press and both, unfortunately, out of print]. Hengel is one of the world's top experts on the socio-political background of the Bible from intertestamental times through the earliest Christian centuries, and so is eminently qualified to tell us the story of two Jewish revolutions. The first—a century or more before Jesus—was the Maccabean revolt against Hellenistic oppressors (the Seleucids). The second—getting underway during the time of Jesus and running almost fifty years beyond him—was the Zealot revolt against Roman oppression.

However, the ultimate purpose behind Hengel's study is to critique the revolutionist, liberationist, radical-social-change, political-activist theologies of our own day (by which the Brethren have been so strongly affected). "Revolution" we can here define as "an all out, human-heroic effort to unseat an evil regime (the Establishment) and replace it with a just one (the Revolution)." The word "violence" does not appear in this definition; but the big question is whether a revolution (in this sense) has any possibility of success without resorting to at least some forms of violence. Thus, to avoid confusion, Hengel is careful not to subsume under "revolution" the way of Jesus; it, of course, is something quite different from human-heroic political effort.

Hengel takes the two Jewish revolutions as models of revolution in general—models regarding idealism and ideology, as well as models of procedure and outcome.

There is no question but that both the Maccabean and Zealot uprisings met every possible qualification for "good," justifiable revolution: (1) In all aspects of life, the populace had been pushed to the extremes of oppression; their grievances were real; they were in despair and without any hopeful alternative. (2) The revolution arose out of the lower classes and was the spontaneous expression of their need. Their leaders came out of their own ranks. They were not being manipulated for the political advantage of any ideological clique. (3) Their goals were entirely right and good. They sought no more than simple justice; their demands were in no way exhorbitant or self-serving. (4) Their religious motivation was strong and pure. They wanted truly to obey God, to be free to worship him, and to establish his justice. They were not prostituting the faith in the service of their revolution. (5) Each of the revolts turned to violence only as a last resort; any observer would have had to agree that no other political possibility was open to them.

The main difference between the two was that the Maccabean revolt succeeded and the Zealot revolt failed. The sad comparison was that both came to the same thing—"success" or "failure," no appreciable difference.

The Maccabees were quickly successful in achieving their

revolutionary goals: they won back the temple and reconsecrated it; they fought themselves free of the Seleucids—their taxation, their enslavement, their cultural hegemony. Yet, in the process, the revolutionists had become power hungry and couldn't bring themselves to stop fighting; in their turn, they became imperialist toward the Gentiles. The revolutionary leadership became corrupt and extortive, fell to fighting among themselves, actually became collaborationist with the Hellenists they had set out to oppose. Perhaps saddest of all, though the revolution originated as resistance to the Jews being forced to give up their faith and become Hellenist, it wound up with the Jewish establishment forcing Gentiles to be circumcised. At the very time Jewish revolutionaries were defeating the Hellenist oppressors, Hellenist morality was subverting Judaism. And it is easy to show that this is not the only revolution in the world to have "succeeded" in just this way.

With the Zealots against Rome, there was also some initial success—a gaining control of at least one section of Jerusalem. But again, the revolutionary leaders fell to fighting among themselves. And in this case, the Roman military responded with a vengeance. The population was killed or went refugee. Jerusalem was leveled to the ground and burned. God's temple was gone forever. And at Masada, the Zealot survivors committed suicide in one of history's most gruesome and ghastly moments. It is no thanks to the heroic freedom fighters that Judaism survived either of these revolutions. Their efforts would have lost it; the survival is owing solely to the grace of God.

Now many Brethren (and other Christians), I think, would say that the only thing wrong in these revolutions was the resort to violence, to methods of carnal warfare. Many proponents of liberation theology would insist that even this was proper—that only establishment violence is wrong but revolutionary violence right and necessary. Few Brethren would go so far; but many do make excuses for revolutionary violence, insisting that it is of an entirely different moral character than establishment violence. Or perhaps they make the same point by really sounding off at establishment violence (notably USA violence) while conveniently failing to notice that of revolutionaries. Listening to the peace people, who would have guessed that the North Vietnamese were doing anything except sitting peacefully in their villages waiting for American bombs to fall on them? The Brethren protest against violence has shown something of a bias.

However, Hengel uses his exercise to show that the style of Jesus is as opposed to that of the revolution as it is to that of the establishment—and this in an entirely fundamental way, not simply on the matter of physical violence. Some liberationist theologians argue that the only reason Jesus doesn't show up as much of a political revolutionary is because the situation of his day didn't really provide for such a role. However, they imply, were he around today, there is no doubt he would be right in there with the best of them.

Hengel's answer is that first-century Palestine showed just as true a revolutionary ferment as any hot spot of the world today; that, had he the inclination, Jesus easily could have joined (and led) the revolution; and that, rather than accidentally missing it, he deliberately disavowed it root and branch.

Personally, I am not confident that, in writing what he did, Hengel fully appreciated what he was on to. But for me, he shows that, in the incident of the tribute money (Mark 12:13-17), Jesus disclosed the very heart of the matter. We will let Hengel explain it his way [*Was Jesus a Revolutionist?*, pp. 32-34] and then I get to say what I think it means. What follows is a paraphrase of Hengel; perhaps my English can communicate a bit better than his German translation can:

Jesus had nothing good to say about the Zealot revolutionaries, although he was probably even more strongly opposed to the Jewish establishment that was cozying up to the Romans. However, Jesus' stating that the tax coin should be given to Caesar in no way can be taken as his siding with the establishment. The question about tax payment had been put to him as the hypocritical trick of some establishment-types. They knew he would never align himself with them, would never favor collaboration. So if they could work him into a corner where he would have to say that taxes should be withheld, he would be as much as an admitted Zealot. Then they could report him to the Roman authorities as being such, an enemy of the state.

The Zealots, it must be understood, were much more than simple tax withholders. Because the tax coin, the Roman silver denarius, bore the picture and inscription of Caesar, they considered it both traitorous and idolatrous for Jews even to have the things. To so much as hold them and profit by them was itself a collaboration with the pagan oppressor. And the revolutionaries were as ready to show their loyalty to God by knifing a Jewish collaborator as a Roman overlord.

That Jesus had to ask for such a coin surely is meant to show that he didn't own one and, to that extent, might qualify as a Zealot. Conversely, that the questioners immediately could produce one clearly identifies them with the establishment. The setup poses an inevitable choice: either the establishment or the revolution.

Jesus' first answer is to the effect that those who are conscientiously able to take money *off* Caesar (his image on the coin is proof enough as to where it came from) had better find themselves also conscientiously able to pay back the share he demands; that is part of the bargain they already have made; they are committed. (Notice, however, that this has nothing to do with the either/or choice. Collaborators should pay their taxes; but that says nothing as to whether one should or should not be a collaborator.)

The zinger comes with Jesus' second answer (which is not an answer to the question that was put); and it is this the text tells us left them "amazed." "How did he manage to get out of that one?" Hengel suggests that the Greek of the connective should be translated as "but" in place of the usual "and": "Render to Caesar the things that are Caesar's — *but* to God the things that are God's."

With that, the whole debate about what does or does not belong to Caesar becomes irrelevant in view of the nearness of God. Choosing God is all that really matters — not the choosing between the establishment and the revolution. All choices other than choosing God become what Hengel calls "adiaphora," i.e., things of no real consequence. It is senseless to take them too seriously, either positively or negatively. Neither the establishment nor the revolution, neither paying taxes nor withholding them has anything to do with the coming of the kingdom of God.

"World power [whether establishment or revolutionary] is neither justified nor condemned. It is deprived of its significance, however, through that little word *but,* which pushes everything to God's side. True freedom from the powers [revolutionary as well as establishment] *begins* with an *inner freedom;* and inner freedom, in the New Testament sense, only he achieves who has grasped in faith the nearness of the love of God which leads him away from himself to his fellow man."

The above is Hengel—slightly elaborated. But this present paragraph is my footnote, to care for a side issue with which Hengel did not concern himself: I think he has it right in interpreting Jesus to say that tax payment or withholding is neither here nor there. Still the fact of the matter is that—both at this point and wherever else in the New Testament taxes are mentioned—the counsel is that they be paid rather than withheld. Does this, then, contradict Jesus' making the matter an adiaphoron and, instead, put tax payment back into the status of a law of God—a law that in fact demands that one always choose the establishment over the revolution? I think not—and would call attention to the instance in which Jesus suggests that a tax be paid in order "not to give offense" (Mt. 17:27). This, it would seem to me, is not to say that we *must* pay our taxes *as unto God* but that—precisely because neither establishment paying nor revolutionist withholding has anything to do with the kingdom of God—the part of wisdom is to pay them, simply to avoid causing offense, i.e., to keep from exacerbating the political conflict that is being given a way too much significance already.

Indeed, it is a matter of record (New Testament record) that, whereas the church today tends to make the socio-political-military situation the crux both of history and the faith, the early church, quite otherwise, developed its tradition and wrote its scriptures right through and across the just as critical juncture of the Jewish-Roman War—yet all the while reading both history and faith as being governed by the will of God instead of the adiaphora of human politics and circumstance.

It was, of course, the Roman wolf that ravaged (and as much as nuclearized) Palestine there in the first century. Yet, the Zealots themselves have to take much of the blame for what happened. They deliberately called out the monster. They knew very well that they had not the wherewithal to repulse him. But, as Hengel makes clear, they were entirely confident that, if they aroused him to expose his full evil, God would intervene to put him away — such was their messianic expectation. The trouble, of course — as so often — was that God was not standing where they were sure they had him. But anyone who calls out evil to make it show itself (whether in the newspapers or anywhere else) must share responsibility for whatever mayhem results. And that well may be why, in the tradition that spans right across that Jewish-Roman War, the New Testament writers counsel Christians not to join the Zealots but to pay their taxes *to that very same Roman wolf* — in order not to cause offense, in order not to resist one who is evil, in order not to ignite violence but to pacify it.

Hengel's insight into the Mark 12 passage has brought us this far; now we are on our own.

What Jesus has accomplished here, I would suggest, is to distinguish the one, ultimate, absolute choice from all lesser, relative choices. So draw on your mental blackboard, if you will, a short horizontal line. As poles of the either/or choice, label one end THE ESTABLISHMENT and the other THE REVOLUTION. You need not go to the mental effort of writing them in; but consider that subhead labels could be "Collaborate with the Romans" at the one end and "Resist the Romans" at the other; "Conscientiously Pay Taxes" at the one end and "Conscientiously Withhold Taxes" at the other. And a little thought will show that, in addition to "The Establishment vs. The Revolution," there are any number of other moral polarities that would fit the diagram as well. Any and all such horizontal alignments — such human alternatives — we will call "relative choices."

But Jesus says that none of these is really where it's at; they are one and all "adiaphora" in comparison to the choice that truly counts. So, at the other end of your blackboard (you haven't already erased that first diagram, have you?) draw a vertical line — except don't let it be a solid line (dots, or dashes, or other forms of tenuousness will do). At the top of that line, then, write GOD. At the bottom we want to put the entire "Establishment vs. Revolution" alignment, plus any and all other horizontalities — and summarize the whole schmeer with the word WORLD.

Now this vertical alignment—in which a person either chooses "God" or else chooses something that, however good or evil it may seem, is obviously "not-God"—this constitutes the only ABSO-LUTE choice there is or can be. It is what Jesus was talking about when he said: "The eye is the lamp of the body. So, if your eye [namely, this choice] is sound, your whole body will be full of light; but if your eye is not sound, your whole body will be full of darkness. If then the light in you is darkness, how great is the darkness! No one can serve two masters; for either he will hate the one and love the other, or he will be devoted to the one and despise the other. You cannot serve God and mammon" (Mt. 6:22-24). It is the idea the book of Revelation is after in insisting that, at any given moment, each person bears either, on his forehead, the seal with the name of the Lamb and his Father/or else, on his hand, the mark with the name of the Beast.

This choice is "absolute" in that everyone must make it; to fail to choose God is already to have chosen the World. Of no "relative choice" is that the case; the whole point of Jesus' response to the tax question is that failure to join the Revolution is NOT the equivalent of joining the Establishment (or vice versa). The assumption that one must either absolutize the state as a god (as does the establishment) or else absolutize it as a satan (as does the revolution) is utterly false. Jesus asks us to absolutize God alone and let the state be the human relativity it is, at once relatively good and relatively evil —even as you and I are.

The choosing of God—and only this choice—is "absolute" in that everything else hangs on it. Only here does "your whole body" become full of either light or darkness.

This choice is "absolute" in that it is the only one truly "black and white"—or "light and dark" (reading the vertical from the top down). There is no connection, no possibility of continuity, no shadings of gray, no middle ground, nothing in common between the two ends of the choice (which is why, on your diagram, you were asked to make the vertical a non-line). Here and only here are we invited—or even permitted—to "hate the one and love the other, be devoted to the one and despise the other."

This choice—and only this choice—is "absolute" in that there is no room for dialog or discussion between the poles, for seeking what is true and good in each, for effecting any sort of reconciliation or compromise. Here there can be no conversation, for when God is that which is to be chosen, "To whom then will you compare me?"—as he puts it in Isaiah 40:25. All one can do is to *choose* and choose *absolutely*—"Let goods and kindred go; this mortal life also."

Now the root sin of "zealotism" is the desire to absolutize what are actually relative choices, to treat as vertical those alignments that are actually horizontal. The contest between two different "not-God" positions is presented as though it involves a choosing of "God," as though one of the positions were the position of "God" and the other that of "not God."

Yet, the truth of the matter is that a relative choice represents an entirely different alignment from the absolute choice and must be treated in an entirely different manner. God has the right to demand that every person choose him or, in failing to do so, choose the world. We have no right to demand that anyone choose between our humanly-defined alternatives. Being humanly defined, the alternatives we set up are never black and white; at best, they are only differing shades of gray. We have no right, then, to suggest that people must choose what we define as "the Revolution" or else be damned as part of what we define as "the Establishment," choose what we define as "liberalism" or else be damned as what we call "a conservative," choose what we define as "peacemaking" or else be damned according to our definition of "a warmaker."

Just the contrary of the way it is with the absolute choice, relative choices—in their comparative grayness—must recognize the essential commonality of the two poles. Both the Revolution and the Establishment are nothing more than human ideologies regarding the use of political power; either may be capable of making some real contribution to human welfare, and each is capable of really messing up things. Neither guarantees anything, whether good results or bad ones. Establishment-types are sinners and revolutionaries are sinners—you can take that as axiomatic. Consequently, what horizontal alignments present as "opposite poles" are actually different points on a spectrum of relative good and evil (which is why you drew your horizontal as a solid, continuous line).

Thus, just where the vertical, absolutist alignment emphasizes polarization and prohibits conversation, horizontal relativism calls for the opposite. What it presents as polar distinctions are not such and dare not be treated as such. Instead, what is called for from both ends is humility, honesty, openness — a spotting what is wrong and a looking for what is right in both the one and the other, a mutually critical and affirmative give-and-take, two-way recognition and correction, a search for reconciliation through the discovery of new locations on the spectrum where the values of each can be preserved even as the poles move closer together. Precisely because the alignment is "relative," each position must be treated as only relatively right or wrong, relatively fixed, relatively important.

Kierkegaard, perhaps, has put it best: "Whatever difference there may be between two persons, even if humanly speaking it were most extreme, God has it in his power to say, 'When I am present, certainly no one will presume to be conscious of this difference, because that would be standing and talking to each other in my presence as if I were not present'" [*Works of Love,* p. 315].

However, just because — in comparison to the absolute choice, in comparison to God and his kingdom — these relative choices are seen as adiaphora is not to say that they are of no importance at all, that they merit no concern or attention from us. To say that each pole represents a shade of gray is not to say that, in every case, each is the same shade, that there may not be a relative advantage of one over the other which is worth striving for. Jesus never condemns our involvement in and struggle with relative choices; in fact, he gives instruction and counsel regarding many of them. But what he does condemn is our bypassing the absolute choice in the interests of absolutizing some relative choice which we choose to make all-important. Thus, we cannot, in principle, declare that the Revolution is always preferable to the Establishment (or vice versa). Each case is *relative* to its own merits.

We are now to the place, then, that we can define "zealotism" as "that moral zeal which gets so carried away in its own 'good cause' that it confuses its own relative righteousness as being the absolute righteousness of God himself." The anti-Roman Zealots of the first century are a good example of the disease; but we need to realize that, even there, "zealotism" was not confined to the Zealots. The collaborationist Jewish establishment, for its part, was just as zealously certain that *it* represented the "God pole" of the alignment. And each could adduce good arguments. The establishment held the temple, the priesthood, the scriptures, and religious learning—and stood for law and order. The revolution represented the eschatological hopes of the people—and stood for righteousness, justice, and the liberation of the poor. The fact that each had a convincing God-claim would seem a rather good indicator of the relativity of both. And Jesus displayed the very wisdom of God when, rather than choosing between them, he renounced the zealotism of both.

Yes, zealotism can and does show itself across the spectrum; it is nothing peculiar to the radical Left. In our day, for instance, the Moral Majority shows as much absolutizing zeal as anyone. But because books scoring that Moral Majority are already a dime a dozen (true, they do cost more than that; but they are as many as that), I shall continue to speak to the Brethren and the less-noted zealotism of our end of the horizontal.

If our analysis is correct, the Zealot movement did not *become* sinful only when it became violent. In its absolutizing of the relative, it was sinful from the word "go" and would have been so even it if had somehow managed to avoid violence. In fact, my guess is that it is the very action of absolutizing that makes violence as much as inevitable. Once a party is convinced that it represents God over against Satan, it is in position to justify whatever proves necessary in taking out that satan.

The sin of absolutizing the relative could, I suppose, be called "idolatry"; but I am not sure that quite says it. It is not so much a case of setting up a god besides Yahweh as it is our presuming to locate God, to say where he stands (namely, at the position of our good cause and against the other party's bad cause). We do this rather than allowing him to locate us (namely, as sinful, lost, and helpless). But whatever such sin should be called, it is bad—a form of Eden's "titanism" in which man presumes to set the rules by which God must play, to assert his own human wisdom and piety over against that of God himself. Zealotism signifies something much more serious than simply an enthusiasm for God that accidentally overdoes a good thing.

Starting out bad, zealotism inevitably gets worse. We defined it as "moral zeal for a good cause" — but that was to put the matter as charitably as possible. With some regularity, zealotism comes across more strongly as "moral zeal against a bad cause." Although the first-century Zealots *claimed* (undoubtedly honestly enough) that their motivation was the liberation of the poor, what they became best at was sticking it into the ribs of the rich (to the extent that they even came to be known as "the knifemen"). And true to form, contemporary zealots prove much more proficient at denouncing whomever they see to be warmakers than they are at positive peacemaking.

Now it may be thought that these two — loving the good and hating the evil — come to the same thing, that they are simply two sides of the same coin; but that just isn't so. Jesus showed us that they are not — at the same time showing that he was not a Zealot. He loved the poor — but did it without hating the rich. He loved the poor, indeed, while showing love toward different rich people at the same time — which is not to deny that he also recognized a relative distinction between the two. And how did he manage it? He managed it by keeping relative alignments relative, refusing to absolutize them. It is only those absolutely sure of their own rightness who can afford to take after those they know to be absolutely wrong.

Indeed, there is reason to believe that, at least in some cases, behind the zealous castigation of a particular sin or sinner lies the castigator's need to enhance his own righteousness. He centers in on a selected sin (which is not his) in the interests of promoting his own selective righteousness. This clearly was the case with the scribes and Pharisees whose zealous hatred of immorality had them ready to kill the woman taken in adultery. Their true concern was not so much her sin as their righteousness. They were out to use her (perhaps not totally unlike her partner in adultery) — by absolutizing her relative moral defect as a way of simultaneously absolutizing their own (defective) moral righteousness. The black-and-white thinking of zealotism lends itself to such grotesquery: the black, black, blacker I can paint my selected enemy, the white, white, more heroic white it leaves me. "I thank God that I am not as other men."

In this regard, there is at least one conspicuous difference between all biblical theologies on the one hand and contemporary liberationist theologies on the other—whether those target Third World poverty (liberation theology), racism (black theology), sexism (feminist theology), or war (peace theology). Even if modern versions of biblical thought have to be stigmatized as "Western-white-male-military theology," it nevertheless must be admitted that this theology is dedicated to helping Western, white, male warmakers (along with everyone else) find out and face up to their own sinfulness. But with the liberationist theologies, the regular pattern is to find out and denounce the sin of the enemy and leave one's own constituency smelling like a rose. Zealotism simply does not make for good biblical theology.

Beyond doubt, the preferred target for current Brethren zealotism is "nuclear warmaking" (according to our own definition of that term, it must also be said). Our literature and teaching give the distinct impression that we consider it more important for a person to join us in opposing the nukes than in joining us in the worship of Jesus Christ as Lord and Savior. We use, as a truer test of a person's Christianity, his stand on nuclear arms than his stand on the biblical proclamation as to who Christ is—although the Bible itself hardly permits us to define the faith as simply an antiwar movement.

In our tunnel-visioned zealotism, we are totally sensitive to the selected "sin of the day" (which is regularly someone else's rather than our own) and almost totally insensitive to, say, the sin of biblical-theological carelessness of which this book speaks. But in making my thought as pointed as possible, allow me to become entirely specific by speaking of a sin which is truly a closer parallel to warmaking.

In the same list of commandments in which is found "You shall not kill" is the one which reads "You shall not commit adultery"—and there is nothing in the text indicating that the list can be differentiated into those sins which are really, really bad and those which aren't really bad at all.

That paragraph sets my argument but does not constitute it; there is a great deal more that needs to be said. Surely, in evaluating the "sinfulness" of a given behavior, the criterion cannot be simply the statistical-technological one of how many people are adversely affected in what way. Much more important is the discovery of the spiritual economy involved, what the sin has to say regarding one's relationship to God. "Sin" always is defined in relation to God before it is in relation to neighbor (though I do not mean to suggest that the two elements are ever separable). Yet, our modern tendency is to completely overlook the Godward aspect of sin.

However, in the present case, the prior and essential sinfulness of nuclear armament is the effrontery of the nations in wresting from God's hands the power and authority to direct the course of history and decide the future of the planet. It is the Tower of Babel all over again. And by the way, this has been the sinfulness of militarism since the beginning. Nuclear capability marks a technological advance but hardly a qualitative leap in the spiritual economy of the sin itself. The sinfulness of the human heart has been a constant throughout the life of the race. Certainly scripture gives us no license to absolutize one sin, one sinner, or one particular instance of sin over all others.

"But are you suggesting that adultery can be compared to war?" I am. I am not out to prove that being unfaithful to one's wife is as bad as killing her, though there may be cases in which the consequences are much the same. Rather, I want to analyze one particular form of adultery for its spiritual significance. So I am not talking about the adultery of a single, short-lived affair. I am speaking of habitual, unrepented promiscuity on the part of people in high places.

President Lyndon Johnson gets us to the core of the problem. I understand that a recent biography makes it plain that he was one of those of whom we speak; and it also quotes him as saying something to the effect that "power" is a wonderful aphrodisiac. So when we talk about adultery — this sort of adultery — we actually are talking about an individual's sense of personal power. And my observation of different cases — most from a newspaper distance, but some from closer at hand — convinces me that Johnson was telling it like it is.

The Bible is the place to find our confirmation. Although, as far as we know, King David's was a one-time affair that was quickly repented, yet we must be impressed by how seriously God took the matter — sending a prophet especially to get things straightened out and having the story written up in scripture as a crucial juncture in the history of God's people. Plainly, more was involved than simply God's legalistic displeasure in having one of his commandments broken.

No, with David—as with probably most of his colleagues in this sin—it seems not to have been his intention to challenge the Seventh Commandment. In fact, he probably was all for it . . . as a rule for common, run-of-the-mill sinners. They need such constraint; it helps keep them on the straight and narrow. But His Royal Majesty, King o' the Realm David, Exalted Excellence and Lord of All He Surveys? Now that's different. It is given to kings to *make* the laws—certainly not to *obey* them along with the hoi polloi. It's matter, I guess, not so much of "executive privilege" as of "titanic privilege," the privilege of being "big man."

Thus, David's sin was not so much "adultery" as the pretension of claiming to be "like God," of grasping the Johnson-truth that "power" is not only a wonderful aphrodisiac but also the invitation and license to use it. God well understood what was involved and so had the affair commemorated as marking both David's personal decline and the eventual breakup of his kingdom. If the spiritual economy of nuclear armament is that of Babel, the spiritual economy of this sort of adultery is that of Eden; and who would presume to say which is worse?

So when it is known that the practice of one of the most acclaimed Christian heroes of our day was nearer that of Lyndon Johnson than of King David (i.e., longstanding habit that was never called to account, stopped, or repented) and was apparently of the same power-proud economy, what are we to think? And hear me well when I say my concern is not so much with the actions of that one adulterer as with the attitude in which the Christian public has accepted his adultery.

"As long as the man was right on peace and brotherhood, anything else should be overlooked." Having already lost our sense of the absoluteness of God, we don't mind that our heroes absolutize themselves a bit; it's part of their heroism. Yet, if warmaking is the state's absolutizing of itself, this style of adultery is a person's absolutizing of himself—the state's action being perhaps the more excusable in that its warmaking can also represent a legitimate desire to protect the people for whom it is responsible.

As both Jacques Ellul and Martin Hengel have observed, within its own secular frame of reference, violence is entirely *necessary* for the state (which is not for a moment to say it is *right)*. Yet I doubt that it ever will be seriously argued that adultery is *necessary* for anyone.

Do you see that our tolerance (and even approval) of individualistic titanism could spell the collapse of civilization just as surely as nuclear weaponry might? Is not the zealotism of selective sin-sensitivity itself a moral danger? Will we not be held accountable if we foster our own righteousness by absolutizing our enemy's sin of nuclear armament at the very time we are excusing our friend's sin of power-proud adultery? That looks suspiciously like what the Bible calls "casting the first stone." (No, I am not suggesting that, instead of nuclear armament, we ought now absolutize adultery. I am proposing that we move entirely out of zealot absolutizing and that both militarism and adultery be seen as relative to and in continuity with the personal sinfulness of which each of us is guilty.)

With the absolutist zeal that sees moral issues solely in black-and-white comes the license also to say about the opposition anything that pops into your head — as long as it is bad. The assumption seems to be that it is manifestly impossible to malign the devil — whether that devil be the US Government or the National Council of Churches. But regularly, one of the first casualties of zealotism (and a most serious loss) is the biblical command to "speak the truth in love" (Eph. 4:15).

That command has two aspects, both of which are essential. "To speak the truth" surely intends a scrupulous regard for fact — both in taking pains to get the facts (all the facts) before presuming to speak and in sticking to the facts when one does speak. And clearly, this obligation is even more weighty when we set out to accuse an enemy than when we set out to compliment a friend. We need to be aware of and correct for our own emotional bias.

To speak that truth "in love," then, adds a further obligation. Kierkegaard once pointed out that, although our natural propensity is to be very strict toward other people's sins and very lenient toward our own, scripture would have it the other way around: we should be most suspicious of our own self-righteousness and most ready to forgive and make allowance for what we perceive as the sin of others. Of course, he is getting us back to Jesus' instruction about the speck- and log-filled eyes.

But it is in his treatment of "Love Hides the Multiplicity of Sins (1 Peter 4:8)" [In *Works of Love,* pp. 261ff.] that Kierkegaard gets most pointed. One of his theme statements reads: "Love hides the multiplicity of sins, for what it cannot avoid seeing or hearing, it hides in silence, in a mitigating explanation, in forgiveness." And it is his middle term, "a mitigating explanation," that is particularly germane to our topic of speaking the truth *in love.*

In almost every case, even after the facts are in hand and have been given their true value, there is still a great deal of leeway, still room for a number of different interpretations, differing explanations of what the facts actually *mean.* Zealotism, out of its absolutist need to make the black/white contrast as stark as possible, regularly goes for the most negative explanation. Love, Kierkegaard insists, always opts for the most positive. Of course he is not asking that we ignore or twist the facts in the interests of love — rather, in telling the truth, we should make it as loving as the facts will allow.

In coming to specific examples, we will stay by the peace issue as our best example of Brethren zealotism — although the reader should have no difficulty in transposing the analysis to other issues as well. I will take my specimens from both Brethren and non-Brethren literature; but I will not identify the sources. I am concerned that we not target individuals but rather become aware of the spread of this disease of the spirit which infects not only Brethrenism but wide reaches of the church at large.

Let me say at the outset that I believe very few if any peace zealots, of whatever persuasion, to be deliberately unloving speakers of untruth. Recall that our initial definition of zealotism included the words "carried away"; and this must be the very truth regarding these obviously well-intentioned people — whether of the Left or of the Right (including even the first-century Zealots and their Establishment enemies). Nevertheless, zealotism often fails to speak the truth (whether in love or not) and that by several different means.

Half-truth: we seek out and speak loudly the worst things

about the enemy, while neglecting to as much as mention the good things that would round out and balance up his picture.

Half-truth: we single out our selected villain and really roast him, carefully ignoring the fact that, if he were compared to those around him, he might even show up as the best of the bunch.

Half-truth: as per the suggestion Kierkegaard already has made, we give the worst possible interpretation to what may even be accurate facts about our enemy.

Half-truth: we keep the probing spotlight fixed on him and are careful not to let it fall upon ourselves.

Regarding the peace issue, the enemy surely should be identified as that nationalistic pride and pretension which proposes to take over and run things its own way, in defiance of God, the public welfare, and humane concern. But at the same time, it should be recognized that this disease is and has been endemic to every state or government that has ever been. More, it is a disease that can and does infect individuals as well as nations. It has not been demonstrated that even zealots themselves are immune to it.

But zealotism cannot be content with such targeting; the villain has to be more narrowly selected. Nationalistic warmaking now is seen to be the particular sin of the technological West.

With that, absolutism is taking over, and the truth we are committed to speaking is slipping away. Both historically and presently the Third World has warred and killed with all its limited technological skill — just as the West has with its almost unlimited technological skill. But that wars of the Third World have been notably smaller than those of the West is no credit to those peoples' moral restraint — any more than the grand scale of Western wars is a sign of those peoples' greater depravity. Both are intent on doing the best sinning they can with what they've got. And the more I learn about Pol Pot's purge in Cambodia, the more I wonder whether any Western state will ever be able to play in that Third World league. To damn Western war and leave the Third World looking like peacemakers simply is not speaking the truth.

But with zealotism, things get worse rather than better. It turns out that the black heart of the black West is the United States of America. "More than any other event in history the worldwide human experience of those August days in 1945 [Hiroshima and Nagasaki] was a recapitulation of the primeval Fall." In the totality of human history there has been but one sin to compare with Adam's, and our own United States of America has the honor of having committed it. We win out over the Babylonian destruction of Jerusalem, Judas' betrayal of Jesus, the crucifixion of Jesus, the Roman destruction of Jerusalem, the Turkish genocide of Armenia, the Nazi Holocaust, Stalin's purges, you name it. Compared to us, everything else is innocence.

But why would it not be nearer to speaking the truth in love to say some things such as these: "In World War II, every combatant that possessed atomic capability used it. That some did not possess it was sheer accident; the evidence is that all wanted it and would have used it if they had had it — as would the Romans if they could have had it in the first century. So where is this quantum jump in moral evil?"

"Whereas Hiroshima was destroyed with a single bomb, other cities in other nations and other wars have suffered similar devastation from conventional (if not primitive) weapons — it just took a bit longer. So where is the quantum jump in moral evil?"

"Although we are not obligated to agree, we are obligated to give serious consideration and a careful response to President Truman's rationale for using the bomb. He has considerable logic behind him."

One characteristic of zealotism is to pooh-pooh and airily dismiss — rather than face and confute — arguments from the other side. But Truman's stated purpose was to end the war quickly and thus save great numbers of both Japanese and American lives which very surely would have been lost if we had had to fight our way into Japan and Tokyo. Simply to accuse him of a quantum jump in moral evil is neither truthful nor loving. [Hint: I don't think Truman's argument can be rebutted out of the secular logic of the situation itself. It takes the Christian (and thus politically irrelevant) logic that, if we had trusted God, he could have brought events out right without our resorting either to atomic or any other kind of bombs.]

"That the Hiroshima bomb was not what the zealots make it out to be is shown clearly by its context. The bomb was not used as a first strike but as one blow in a raging war in which every combatant was already throwing everything he had. And this war the US had not started but had entered only under the provocation of what was indeed a dastardly first strike. The US purpose in using the bomb clearly was to achieve a surrender and a cessation of hostilities, not a genocide of the Japanese people. In defeating the Japanese, the US did not practice the sort of torture and atrocities the Japanese had practiced very freely in their turn. The subsequent occupation of Japan shows for a fact that the US had no imperialistic designs and no interest in the sort of domination and exploitation that was the case, say, in the Roman occupation of first-century Palestine."

Now I am opposed to war—all war, including the US involvement in World War II. But I find my Bible suggesting that, from Cain on, all war has been very much the same, a manifestation of the same spirit of sin, no matter who is doing it how. What I do not find is this zealot business of playing sides, picking out one party as the particular villain while letting others off as comparatively innocent, using technological advance as the measure of moral regression. And for the life of me, I don't see how this polarizing approach improves our chances of gaining peace. I'll take speaking the truth in love every time. In fact, it strikes me that the only statement in the vein of the opening quotation that scripture would allow is: "I can't speak for others, but I have looked into my own heart and know that, in myself, I have recapitulated the primeval Fall."

It was very interesting for me to discover that, what is to my mind the one best answer and refutation to this sort of anti-Western, anti-American zealotism, was written by a scholar who is himself the sharpest in spotting social, political, and spiritual sin— a man frequently quoted by the peace zealots themselves. The Christian social analyst, Jacques Ellul, a Frenchman, has made the point much better and more authoritatively than I can in an essay, "The Defense of the West," from his book, *The Betrayal of the West.*

Another example of the zealotism Ellul and I deplore is this from a Bible scholar arguing the case for tax resistance and having some trouble with Paul's word that we should pay our taxes, honor the Emperor, and all that. "It should be clear [he says] that it does not do simply to quote Paul as if the nuclear situation and the modern state were no different than the Roman occupation forces."

I contend that man now has bigger trouble than he had before he spoke. He does not see the implication; but as a conservative biblicist, he has lost his authoritative Bible. There is no reason why the logic of his statement could not be worded to read, "It should be clear that it does not do simply to quote the New Testament about the resurrection of Jesus when modern man knows that resurrections cannot and do not occur." But more, what under the sun could this writer come up with if he were called upon, speaking the truth in love, *to document* such a categorical moral superiority of the pagan Roman military over the modern US Government that, inspired by God, the Apostle Paul would be impelled to reverse his word, commanding us to obey the one but disobey the other? The very way the US Government handles *this particular writer's* own tax resistance, compared to the way Rome handled tax resistance in its day, shows that he has his moral comparison wrong end to. Ellul's sharp question would seem to apply: "Is anyone really unable to see the difference between the United States and Hitler or Stalin?" Our Bible scholar is, without doubt, a learned and honest man; I think he simply got "carried away."

But more than just historical distortion is involved in this peace zealotism. I earlier said something to the effect that the stated issue is "war" or "peace" *as the zealots themselves choose to define those terms.* What I had in mind is this: A great many honest Christians see themselves as devoted wholly to peace — even while believing that nuclear deterrence is the only possible way to preserve it. But in our moral zeal, we are not about to allow people of that sort onto the white end of the polarity along with ourselves. We will credit neitther their honesty nor their sincerity; they are warmakers as black as any.

Yet, surely the truth of the matter is that they are as sincere in their desire for peace as are any of the zealots. And they are not fools; their argument deserves a careful hearing. After all, it is true that deterrence has already succeeded in preventing nuclear holocaust for much longer than early predictions said it could. Now I happen also to think that their argument is flawed; and I would like to talk with them about that. But what is certain is that this crucial dialog can't take place as long as, in our zealotism, we feel it necessary to reject these conversational partners out of hand as being no different from evil warmakers.

What may be an even worse violation of speaking the truth in love is our righteous zeal in refusing to recognize any moral distinction between *having* nuclear weapons and the *using* of the same. As one writer has it: "Even if Cain, because of some fear, had held back the lethal blow and had contented himself with murder fantasies and pantomimes when Abel's back was turned, the ghastliness of his intent would have remained. With megakill, too, an unspeakable ghastliness of intent for a hundred-million fold murder is there."

I have some difficulty with this scenario. Cain, the tenor of the account makes plain, is the United States of America; but can the Soviet Union be cast as an innocent Abel with his back turned? But it is even more important that we here apply the test of speaking the truth *in love*. In this case, the "truth," the fact of the matter, is, of course, that these two world powers have a plentitude of nuclear weapons aimed at each other but that the use of them has been restrained up to the present time. Is it not, then, an instance of putting the worst possible construction on those facts when the only motive for restraint that gets mentioned is a fear of retaliation, with presumably all proponents of nuclear deterrence being accused of entertaining murder fantasies and pantomimes — just looking for an opportunity to push the button and gloat in the death of humanity?

Of course, if deterrence is to work at all, it must be accompanied by every sort of tough, extravagant talk (at which, by the way, the zealots are as good as is the establishment). Richard Nixon, for instance, recently was quoted to the effect that he never had given consideration to using nuclear weapons in Vietnam, but that it was not entirely accidental if Saigon got the impression he might. Yet, who knows how many presidents of the United States — and even Russian dictators — have made a private pact with themselves, or with God, never to push the button under any circumstances? That seems to me every bit as likely as the suggestion that they all have been just drooling for the chance to do it.

But what simply cannot be right is for us to join the first-century Zealots in their identifying their own small party as the locus of white-godlikeness and consigning everyone else to the black-demonism outside. As they wound up knifing even those fellow Jews who they decided were collaborators, so we wind up damning as murderers many fellow Christians who are as concerned for peace as we are but who happen not to share quite our view of the matter. Finally, even as I find zealotism unbiblical and unchristian, I can't figure out how it is supposed to work, how it shows any possibility of accomplishing its declared purpose. For instance, a tax-resister publishes an article arguing his position and winds it up by telling the reader, "I fully expect that you will be able to put me down with theological arguments, or discredit me with a self-righteous application of Scripture taken out of context to justify and rationalize your position." What does he hope to gain with such a line?

I suppose there must be some satisfaction in being so sure of your position that you can brand all dissenters as frauds without even hearing what they have to say. I can see a certain cathartic effect for an author, coming on as the White Knight to take his whacks at the foulest monster of human history since the serpent in Eden. I would guess that zealot literature goes great in zealot circles. Of course, it does nothing to encourage one's fellow zealots in examining themselves, looking for their own sin; but it certainly must serve to confirm them in the righteousness of their cause and the wrongness of everyone else's. But I would think the cause of peace (perhaps above all others) should be focused upon reaching out—upon dialoging with others, becoming reconciled with others, attracting others, convincing others, winning others for the peaceable kingdom.

Yet, why should anyone want to consider tax-resistance when told that, if he raises any questions, it can only be that he is putting down the author and self-righteously distorting scripture? This is meant as an invitation to dialog? Why should any believer in peace through deterrence be willing to consider Christian pacifism after being told that he is a murderer awaiting only the opportunity to push the button? Why should anyone consider a peace action when that means accepting the premise that the US is so much more depraved than the Roman military in Palestine that the Bible is to be read the opposite of what it says? Why would any sensible patriot consider aligning himself with the peace movement if it means agreeing that the United States of America committed history's one greatest recapitulation of the Fall of Man? There is no way wild accusation can amount to a positive contribution to the cause of peace. Personally, I doubt whether the irresponsible denouncing of bad people (and I have been denounced by some of the most righteous people around) is ever much help at all—at least it has never been of any help to me. For sure, this was never the mark of Jesus' approach to sinners.

So let us have done with the business of polarizing what ought to be reconciled, denying kinship where we should be finding commonality, shouting down what ought to be heard, putting down those who should be helped up, blackening those who could be made white, making enemies of those who might be made friends, displaying our righteousness at the cost of the other guy's, absolutizing issues that should be left relative, doing violence (yes, "violence") to both "truth" and "love."

So what is the cure? Where is the way out? Jesus said it; and Hengel caught what he said. "But give to God what belongs to God." Make him the "absolute" that shows up all other choices as "relative." That way (and only that way) lies freedom—freedom from false absolutism (whether absolutizing the state as a god or, what is just as bad, absolutizing it as a satan); the freedom to treat relative choices as the human relativities they truly are; the freedom in which "world power is neither justified nor condemned but is deprived of its effect—by giving to God the absolutism that belongs to God."

NOTE: Allow me to emphasize some of the qualifications I have already stated. That I chose to center upon "peace zealotism" is not because I think it is the only one around. It may be that any important cause—and many an unimportant one—develops its own zealotisms; such is the propensity of human advocacy and cause-making. But if I had tried to be "inclusive" regarding zealotisms, this chapter would have taken over the book. Consequently, I chose to be "intensive," in expectation that the reader would have no trouble in spotting the pattern and making the application to other zealotisms far and near.

Likewise, I chose a leftwing zealotism, not because I think zealotism is in any way confined to the Left, but only because

Brethren generally are much more alert to rightwing zealotisms than to those closer to home. But the chapter intends no discrimination regarding zealotism anywhere on the spectrum; each variety is equally bad.

None of the zealots I have known are dishonest, malicious, spiteful people. They are good, sincere, devoted Christians who get "carried away." I can say that from my experience with zealots of the Left. I think we ought to be just as quick to say it regarding zealots of the Right.

CHAPTER SIX

Exhomologesis

My problem is that I will never rate as a theologian, because I don't use enough big words. I intend to rectify the defect at once, by devoting this entire chapter to a discussion of the one word, *exhomologesis*. That needs to take place, even though it necessitates a public confession of my own ignorance in the process.

I first came across "exhomologesis" in a book entitled *Justification* [out of print from Eerdmans] — which title constitutes a rather impressive theological word in itself. The author of *Justification* is a big-word-user of the first rank, Markus Barth, son of the above-but-not-below theologian Karl Barth. In his own right Markus is one of the leading New Testament scholars of our day. However, Markus Barth's book is not actually all that difficult. The really big words are generally confined to the footnotes, the text itself being quite readable.

Justification is a study aimed at discovering what the Apostle Paul wanted to communicate with his use of that word and concept — but on the way it becomes the most exciting and powerful brief presentation of the gospel I know.

Barth uses the word "exhomologesis" at a couple different places in his book; and what really ices it is his saying that "doxology and exhomologesis" are what Paul means by "faith." And yet I had never seen the word before. Now, a true scholar (it is very important for you to understand) is not necessarily one who *knows* all the big words. A true scholar is the person who makes the effort to find out what the big word means when he encounters it. However, let me lead up to that part of the story by recounting how Barth uses the word.

Some scholars would argue that "justification" is the one concept that is most central and basic to Paul's thought; and no scholar would deny that it is at least one of the terms that is central. Barth, then, begins by pointing out that "justification" belongs with a whole batch of other words Paul uses prominently. Along with the noun "justification," there is the verb "to justify" and such other related words as "justice," "judgment," the verb "to judge," and the noun "a judge" (all of the "ju-" words). Although we often fail to recognize the connection, the words "right" and "righteousness" definitely belong with the "justice" words—as does the word "law" (the Old Testament *torah)* and perhaps others. What they have in common is that all come out of a courtroom setting—what Barth calls "a juridical event" (another "ju-" word). And all of this talk must be put back into that context if we are to have any chance of discovering Paul's meaning. So, to understand "justification," we must begin by becoming familiar with courtroom thought and procedure. (And what consequent chapters of this book will make obvious is that—in stark contrast to the modern understanding and proclamation of the faith—not just Paul but the Bible as a whole is simply permeated with juridical metaphor.)

However, what we must not do, Barth insists, is begin by going to a modern Western courtroom, or even a Greek or Roman one. Of course, Paul did have experience in courtrooms from that group—regularly as the defendant and regularly being found guilty. Yet, there is not where he acquired his own legal, courtroom understanding. We dare never forget that Paul was trained as a Jewish rabbi and thus as a student of Old Testament religious law, the torah. He was, by profession, the equivalent of a lawyer (a trained legal mind) within the *Jewish* courtroom context. So Barth properly takes us into the Old Testament to discover what Paul must have meant with his juridical terminology.

That study comes with the force of a revelation, because it turns out that Israel operated out of a courtroom concept entirely different from that to which we are accustomed. Let me outline the distinctions point by point.

(1) Ultimately, there is only one Judge, namely, God [our earlier Micah chapter has direct relevance to this discussion]. Every human judicatory, then, has but one goal, namely, to discover *God's* judgment, submit to it, and apply it as he would have it ap-

plied. God is not only the model but actually the superior and authority of every human judge. The legal process is, thus, essentially a religious action rather than the secular action we have made of it. Obviously, Israel never was able to make the idea work *perfectly*, but at least it was pursued *seriously*.

In scripture, "Judge" is a title and role consistently attributed to God. However, in our thought and worship we have tended to drop it almost entirely—largely, I think, because we don't like the implications. And that, in turn, is because we have never understood what the Bible means by "a judge." So that will be our next point.

(2) In our Western tradition, we tend to think of a judge as a "condemner"; his essential task is to find out guilty parties and punish them. There is, of course—and needs to be—an element of this even in the Hebrew tradition. Yet the primary focus is elsewhere. The judge, now, is one whose first responsibility is to get things set right (according to Judge Jehovah's idea of right, it goes without saying). The judge is preeminently the one to whom the poor, the outcast, and the abused have recourse in order that their situation might be justified, made right. This idea may come as something of a shocker, but Old Testament usage will bear it out: "judge" and "savior" are as much as synonymous terms. And Jesus' parable is right with us: the judge may have turned out to be an unjust one, but the poor widow was correct and knew where she was supposed to go for help.

Accordingly, our whole Pauline word-package speaks much more strongly of making things right, getting them in line with the will of God, than of condemning anyone. And by the way, this interpretation suddenly makes it clear why, in the book of Judges the leaders should be called "judges" even when they are not shown doing anything we would call juridical. They are people through whom God was working to get things set right. So if we are to understand Paul (or any of the biblical writers), we must learn to use "judge" positively as with the Hebrews rather than negatively as with us Gentiles.

(3) The Hebrew judge's responsibility did not end simply with the passing of sentence (no matter how just that sentence might have been). No, it was his responsibility to follow through until the sentence was carried out and right actually done (whether that in-

volved the punishment of the wrongdoer or the restitution of the wronged one or both). In scripture, judging does not begin and end on the bench. Judges are those who *get* things done rather than just saying what ought to be done.

(4) Because the human judge's action is meant to be that of His Honor, Judge Jehovah the Lord, that just decree is to be proclaimed and heralded abroad. The accomplishment of justice is good news and is to be made known. And whenever such is proclaimed, it is expected that every hearer (the defendant, the prosecutor, the parties found guilty, the parties found innocent, the officers of the court, the spectators) every hearer will render personal approval, support, gratitude, and praise. Everyone is involved and should have an interest in the working of justice. And now the matter has been settled. Wrong has been made right. The judge has done the very thing that needed to be done. The affirmation is unanimous. The case is closed.

You see, this response is not simply nice applause but actually a vital aspect of the whole proceeding. Until there is this sort of total affirmation, the judge cannot be said to have *everything* made right — at least not with the holdout who still refuses to recognize that right has been done.

It is at this point Barth says that what all are obliged to render to the judge is "doxology and exhomologesis." "Doxology" I could handle, because I sing it almost every Sunday. However, we need to know that what we sing is only "a doxology," not "the Doxology." *Doxa* is the root that means "glory"; and *-ology* (as in theology, biology, or whatever) means "words about." So "doxology" is words of glory or, more appropriately put, "words of praise." Fine, that figures. But what about "exhomologesis"? It must be something similar; but what?

I hied me to every dictionary (theological and otherwise) in the university library. No help. Likewise, it turned out that none of my learned colleagues on the faculty knew any more than I did. Being without any other recourse, I tried to figure out the meaning from the construction of the word itself. "Ex-" means "out of" (as it did earlier in the word "exists"). The "-homo-" here, I finally realized, does not mean "man" (as in *homo sapiens)* but is rather the "homo" of "homogenized milk," which means "in agreement with" or "of one kind with." The final "-gesis" must be the same as in the word "exegesis"; but I don't know what it means there, either, so not to worry.

"Exhomologesis," I decided, must mean "proceeding out of agreement with." Then I saw it (and still claim I am right, even though technically wrong): "exhomologesis" must be like seconding a motion. Realize, if you will, that the seconder of a motion is in no sense the equivalent of the maker of the motion. They are not Person #1 with a #2 of the same sort coming along behind. The seconder of a motion cannot claim to have thought it up, can't claim it as being his bright idea. No, the most he can do is point to the maker of the motion and say, "Listen to that guy. He's got it right. There's were it's at. And I want to be on public record as recognizing the rightness and justice of the motion *he* made."

So that is the way I have been explaining "exhomologesis" to my students for years. And for all I tell them, they think I know what I've been talking about. Nevertheless, all this time I have been bothered. So not too long back, I came out of class and was walking through the library thinking, "I sure do wish I could find out what 'exhomologesis' really is. I mean, if Barth is correct that it is what Paul intends by 'faith,' it might be important to know." Then suddenly, for the first time ever, it occurred to me that perhaps "exhomologesis" isn't an English word at all but a New Testament Greek word. The word is not italicized in Barth's book—for which somebody deserves my censure. But I got myself to a Greek-English lexicon; in a jiffy I knew the truth, and the truth made me free—free of all the befuddlement in which I had been entangled for years.

Exhomologesis [italicized], I am happy to be able to tell you, is the New Testament word which is regularly translated "confession," "to confess." Keep reading and you will learn its Old Testament Hebrew equivalent in the next chapter. Now I see that Barth freely uses the word "confession" in the same passages where he uses "exhomologesis"; but he didn't have enough consideration to tell us dummies that all in the world he was doing was switching from one language to another.

However, my scholarly following up on the biblical term "exhomologesis" has provided some insights that go even beyond what Barth had to say.

In both Hebrew and Greek—as rather apparently is the case in

English—the word "confession" originated as a juridical term out of the courtroom setting. Where else do confessions get made? Thus, this term belongs right along with the word-package and general metaphor Paul uses. In the Bible, then, as with us, the word has two apparently quite divergent meanings. We can talk about confessing crimes, sins, and wrongdoings. Let's call this the "negative" meaning of the term—although we will later discover its true significance to be anything but negative. On the other hand, we can talk, as Isaiah and Paul do, about every knee bowing and every tongue *confessing* that Jesus Christ is Lord. Let's call this the "positive" sense of the term. So "confess" can be used in either a negative or a positive sense.

While we're here, let's follow up on that Isaiah-Paul reference; it is most instructive. In Philippians 2:10, Paul writes that "at the name of Jesus every knee should bow . . . and every tongue *confess* that Jesus Christ is Lord to the glory of God the Father." Now the strong reference to Jesus Christ of course makes that passage emphatically *Christian*. However, Paul's language and basic idea are not of Christian origin. They are Jewish. Paul is quoting the book of Isaiah. And the 45th chapter of Isaiah is made to order for our purposes.

In verse 20, God says, "Assemble yourselves and come, draw near together, you survivors of the nations!" and in verse 21, "Declare and present your case; let them take counsel together!" Clearly, we are in a courtroom setting, with God the Great Judge launching his final judgment by calling all nations before his bar of justice. In verse 22, he then proclaims, "Turn to me and be saved, all the ends of the earth." Whatever condemnation may be required (and inevitably there is some), nevertheless, the end and goal of God's judgment is "salvation." The courtroom is the place of salvation. The Judge is essentially Savior. And it is by turning to him and accepting his judgment (his making things right) that the world will be saved.

Finally, then, in verse 23, comes the Judge's solemn decree: "By myself I have sworn, from my mouth has gone forth in righteousness a word that shall not return." (The words "sworn" and "righteousness" are still keeping us very much within the courtroom idiom.) Then follows the guarantee: "To me every knee shall bow, every tongue shall swear"—the very line Paul quotes. Now the

RSV has Isaiah use the word "swear" where Paul uses the exhomologesis-word "confess." We undoubtedly are dealing with equivalent expressions in Isaiah's Hebrew and Paul's Greek, for Paul surely knew his Isaiah inside and out and was a competent translator. But God here swears that he is going to perform a righteous judgment that will compel exhomologesis from every tongue, that will inevitably call forth the confession that he is the one just Judge in whose judgment our own salvation is to be found. Paul adds only that that judgment did in fact happen in Jesus Christ. But "confession" is found to fit into the picture precisely where Barth says it should.

So exhomologesis belongs. It has both a negative and a positive aspect. It seems that the negative marked the earlier, original use and that the word then moved over into the positive significance. However, a most important observation is that, even when "exhomologesis" is used positively, the negative sense is never completely absent. In short, when I confess God as Lord (the positive sense), I also am confessing that I am not lord, that I have no lord-qualifications in myself (the negative sense). Thus, in exhomologesis, when a person seconds the motion, he is not only affirming the maker of the motion and crediting him with its rightness, he is also pointing out, "It was not *my* motion; it was *his*. I will not even say that I could have made such a motion. In fact, when the motion-maker is God, I know I could not have."

In effect, then, that first, so-called "negative" action is a necessary clearing of the deck, a getting self out of the way so the total credit and glory can be given to God. Paul as much as says this very thing in 2 Corinthians 4:7, "We have this treasure in earthen vessels, to show that the transcendent power belongs to God and not to us."

Yet, it is on just this point the thinking of our day invariably hangs up. *We* know that the one true "treasure" is the potential of our common humanity. So Paul's formula must be reversed. Well, perhaps not entirely: we do not insist on God's being "an earthen vessel." No, we are willing even that he be "a crystal goblet"—*if* it is kept clear that he exists to serve our human enhancement, that his very reason for being is to help us "accomplish that which is in us."

So it is precisely this negative side of exhomologesis that leads us moderns to get our backs up and refuse to come through with what the Bible indicates is our first and foremost obligation to God. Remember, Barth insists that "doxology and exhomologesis" is what Paul means by "faith." So if there is no confession of God as the righteous Judge, there is no faith in him, either.

Now in this regard, modern man might be willing to give God praise of a sort — if the understanding were that God would respond in kind. We are not unwilling to scratch God's back, as it were, if he will scratch ours in return. But if the pattern must be the negative-positive one of "not me, but thee," then we choose not to participate. Such self-denial and even self-accusation run too counter to the contemporary mood of self-fulfillment and liberation, human heroism, positive self-image, feeling good about ourselves, and the assertiveness training of "I am somebody."

Nevertheless, Barth shows us how Paul incorporates negative-positive exhomologesis right into the heart of the gospel. I must abbreviate Barth's presentation almost beyond recognition; but let me touch the high points. And notice if you will, one of Barth's most valuable insights: Paul's "justification" has reference not so much to the believer's being made right with God (although that is by no means excluded) as to the cosmological, eschatological drama by which the whole creation is being set right. Justification is social and political as well as personal and private.

Humanity as a whole [Paul recounts] is called into the courtroom to face the final judgment of God. There, his righteous decree is that "all have sinned and fallen short of the glory of God and that the wages of sin is death." This decree, then, calls us to make the negative-positive confession which says, "We are sinners deserving of death as you say; but we want also to confess that, even so, you are the one, true, and righteous Judge whose judgment is good and fair and even necessary if things ever are to be made right." (Consider that, unpleasant as the word may be, getting your cancer identified as a cancer is prerequisite to any hope for a cure.)

As the next day's court action, there comes the work of Jesus Christ, centering in his death and resurrection. With this, there is the Judge's new judgment, namely, a "No" to Sin but a "Yes" to Humanity. The Judge now says, in effect: "As guilty, all must die along with Christ; but then, out of grace, I choose also to resurrect them along with him." (Be clear, God is as much "Judge" in this decree as he was in the other; the earlier action was just as truly a "saving" one as this. There has been no change of roles or a reversing of direction. The diagnosing of your cancer and the surgical removal of it are two steps taken by the same doctor in effecting the one cure.) But in this case the negative-positive confession should come back: "We didn't deserve this salvation and never would have thought of doing things this way. We would simply have declared ourselves innocent, which would, of course, have been a lie. So we confess that the way of your judgment has been altogether loving, full of grace and power and truth. All praise to the Judge."

This last event represented the *passing* of the Judge's sentence in favor of man. He now proceeds to follow up and actually *accomplish* it through the return of Christ, the resurrection of the dead, and the consummation of the kingdom—the kingdom in which Sin shall disappear and Humanity be justified into eternal righteousness. And once again, a negative-positive confession is called for: "We didn't deserve any of this; we didn't create any of this; we didn't even do a very good job of cooperating with it. We regularly tried to take over and run things according to our own wisdom. But worthy art thou, O Judge of the Universe, to receive all honor and power and glory and blessing both now and forever more. Amen!"

Notice, then, Paul's one best statement regarding exhomologesis, Romans 10:9-10. It consists of two sentences, the first of which manages to combine exhomologesis, faith, and salvation: "If you *confess* with your lips that Jesus is Lord and *believe* in your heart that God raised him from the dead, you will be *saved.*" The second tops it by going for four: "For man believes [i.e., has faith] and so is justified [i.e., is made right by God], and he confesses [i.e., performs exhomologesis] and so is saved [salvation]." That Paul uses "exhomologesis" to tie into one bundle his other three big concepts—faith, justification, and salvation—shows just how basic this negative-positive confession truly is. (And we might recall that the package from Isaiah 45 included practically the same elements.)

So Barth suggests that this willingness to give the righteous Judge appropriate "doxology and exhomologesis" is what Paul means by "faith" and thus that which God most wants and expects from us. This makes sense. Normally, I would guess, we think of "faith in God" as the equivalent of "trust in God." That is all right;

but exhomologesis includes everything trust does and then goes quite beyond it. Of course, whoever is willing to make this good negative-positive confession about God obviously trusts him. Yet, trust is essentially a "feeling" about God; exhomologesis is a willingness to go beyond simply personal feeling to a putting the matter into solemn, public declaration. Trust is an attitude regarding what God *will* do; exhomologesis includes that but also attests the preeminent rightness of what God already has done and is presently doing. Trust sees God as good but does not emphasize the unique character of that goodness; exhomologesis, by including the specification of our own sin and unworthiness, highlights God's goodness as superlative beyond compare. I, for one, am ready to say that Barth is right and has used exhomologesis to fill out and enrich the concept of faith to which both Paul and the Bible as a whole would call us.

It could be that, in learning what "exhomologesis" means, we have captured the entire argument of this book in one word. Properly understood, that word "exhomologesis" could stand at the heart of our Brethrenism chart and catch up everything we have tried to say. For us, what is the one thing needful? This is it. If we were to gain this one, everything on that chart or in our Goals for the 'Eighties would pretty much come in its train. If we were to gain all the others and have not exhomologesis, they would profit us nothing.

It may be that the picture of God as Judge first enters scripture with Abraham's question of Genesis 18:25, "Shall not the Judge of all the earth do right?" Now that actually is a nonquestioning question, or what is known as a rhetorical question. What it truly is is an invitation to exhomologesis. Spoken there in Genesis or anywhere else, the question compels its own response. "Shall not the Judge of all the earth do right?" "You bet he will! He always has; he always does; he always will. Blessed be the name of the Lord!"

So let us here and now dedicate ourselves to learning and practicing what is positively the best possible positiveness, that of negative-positive exhomologesis. Let us learn it until we *want* to do it as the greatest of all human privileges rather than resist doing it as a demeaning obligation. So learn the pattern: not me, but thee / not my will, but thine be done / not my heroism, but thy glory / not

God's "going my way," but "where he leads me I will follow" / my
sin, thy righteousness / or as Blumhardt perhaps most cogently put
it: our readiness to die (die to everything of self and the sheerly
human) so that Jesus might live.

> Out of my bondage, sorrow, and night,
>   Into thy freedom, gladness, and light . . .
> Out of my sickness into thy health,
>   Out of my want and into thy wealth . . .
> Out of my sin and into thyself,
>   Jesus, I come to thee.

CHAPTER SEVEN

The Theology of Justice

Logic might say that this chapter belongs back with the chapter on Micah 6:8. After all, it does pick up and expand upon the close relationship introduced there between "justice" and "worship." Logic not only *might* but *does* say that this chapter should precede the one on exhomologesis. After all, it does develop the Old Testament theology upon which Paul's "justification/exhomologesis" concept was based. And logic again would say that the proper place for this chapter is right here. After all, for Christians, perhaps the one truest way to read the Bible is to start with the New Testament revelation in Jesus Christ and then *go back* to let the Old Testament fill in and enrich that distinctively "Christian" understanding.

But that's "logic" for you—offering so much help that it makes the decision more difficult rather than easier. So the chapter winds up here for "my" reasons rather than those of "logic." This chapter got itself thought up and written long after the exhomologesis chapter was already fixed in black and white. And it is much easier for me to write so as to build upon and proceed from what I have already written than to play like I don't know what comes next and so write the chapter as though it actually had come first.

Although the study here presented is truly my own, the scholarly resources most helpful in putting it into motion were the works of a British Old Testament scholar, Norman H. Snaith. His essential book is *The Distinctive Ideas of the Old Testament* (Schocken Books). And it is supplemented by his articles— "Judge," "Just," "Justice," and "Righteous"—in Alan Richardson (ed.), *A Theological Word Book of the Bible* (Macmillan). These are recommended for anyone wanting further documentation and a more technical treatment.

Snaith wrote his book some thirty to forty years ago, out of a concern over the even-then-becoming-popular study of comparative religion. He felt very strongly that, in trying to show all religions as being essentially the same, peripheral aspects of the Old Testament were being played up and central aspects ignored. In consequence, it was his opinion that the biblical faith was inaccurately presented. So Snaith set out to identify the elements he found to be both central to the Old Testament faith and, at the same time, entirely distinctive. He did this by spotting a series of crucial Hebrew terms and elucidating the thought that lies behind them. These keywords turn out to be, not a haphazard collection, but a string that forms an integrated thought pattern.

In the following, I use Snaith's string but vary it to suit my own purposes. He provides the scholarly documentation and particularly the translation and definition of the Hebrew words; but the actual Bible study is of my own doing.

I am calling this "the theology of justice," but we need to be clear about what that means. "Justice" is not necessarily the most basic term in the group. Most important, we are not starting from the assumption that we already know what "justice" is, that it already is a recognized and accepted value, and that all that is now wanted is for us to go to the Bible in search of theological legitimation and backing for our idea of "justice." To my mind, this has been the greatest flaw of current "liberation theology." It has taken its start, not from the study of scripture, but from the secular, socially popular idea of "liberation." And thus the liberation theologians came to the Bible with a built-in bias and have searched out (and been ready to find) only as much of the biblical message as fits their preconceived notion of "liberation."

So rather than being a theology we are now to construct around our understanding of "justice," the following is to be a biblical-theological investigation that begins by questioning our modern understanding of the term and so goes to the Old Testament to find out where the idea came from and what the word of God originally intended by it.

Authority/Deference

We start our string with a concept that actually stands prior to

Snaith's starting point. Throughout this study it will be plain that the Old Testament invariably presents God as *the authority* to whom man owes *deference.* I have taken pains in selecting this pair of terms as being most accurate to what wants to be said but also most resistant to the bad implications some people insist on reading into the biblical terminology.

The Old Testament picture of God is coming under a great deal of criticism in our day. The attack upon his "patriarchal masculinity" is not really the issue but only one symptom of a more radical challenge. Accusations regarding such titles as Lord, King, Judge, and Father are part of our pervasive cultural disdain for all notions of "authority" and particularly for the suggestion that we need ever "defer" to anyone. Yet in making their case, the critics are not quite biblically honest. They suggest that these titles all suggest aloofness, distance, coldness, tyranny, domination, superiority, or whatever. What is not quite honest is their giving the impression that all the Old Testament does is to throw out these titles and leave us free to read into them what we will. But the truth of the matter is that scripture proceeds to give a great deal of content and interpretation to every title it proffers. And that content, in every case, turns out to be quite different from what the critics insist is the case.

A little biblical education would stop the mouths of these accusers in a hurry. Certainly, we are obligated to read the Bible for what it means to communicate (and does communicate) and not for the defects we are eager to find. Indeed, just here is a most serious defection from our commitment to use scriptrue as the rule of faith and practice. When, in the supposed superiority of modern wisdom, we undertake to correct and improve scripture to suit our ideas of "truth," we have in effect made ourselves an authority over God himself.

So, in order to defend the Bible against that with which it is falsely impugned and at the same time protect what it is most intent to affirm, I have chosen to speak of divine authority and human deference. A true "authority," we must know, shows none of the character of which the critics complain. An authority is not a peer who has arbitrarily set himself up above others or gained power over them. A true authority is one who does in actuality possess "truth" in a way not found in just everybody else. Thus, my auto mechanic is an authority. He does not impose himself on me, dictate to me, or lord it over me; but I would be a fool not to defer to him regarding what should happen to my car. Indeed, in getting to that truth, one word from the authority is better than the vote of a hundred numbskulls like myself.

Surely there are situations in which it is right to depend upon democratic decision—or even allow each person to do his own thing. But thank God there are also "authorities" for situations in which a vote, or one's own ideas, would have no "truth value" at all. When, for example, it comes to whether I should have an appendectomy, I'll take the authority every time. And if, out of some sort of misguided desire never to admit that I am anything but the greatest, I should refuse to defer to true authority, I am of all men the most to be pitied.

Keep an eye out as we go along; but one thing our study is meant to show is that the Old Testament regularly presents God as the one dependable and absolutely necessary authority for all truth —yet never as any of these other things the critics accuse him of being. Further, our deference to his authority—our exhomologesis, if you will—is seen to be the very essence of faith. So if modern critics succeed in undercutting the authority of God, the result—far from being an updated and improved version of the Christian faith—will actually signal the total loss of that faith. Divine authority accepted in human deference is the foundation of everything we shall learn from here on out.

The Holiness of God, qodesh [ko'-desh]

The word "holy" identifies probably the most basic attribute the Old Testament gives to God. It is its fundamental term for making the point about his authority and our deference. Snaith presents a very detailed history of the word. We will follow instead the simplified and clear presentation from Martin Buber's, *The Prophetic Faith.*

Essentially, *qodesh* identifies God as being *unique,* as being different from, distinguished from, superior to anything and everything else—all of which, in comparison to him, is the ordinary, mundane, customary, and everyday. *Qodesh* is found only in God and does not occur apart from him.

Nevertheless, Buber is quick to insist, it does not follow from

God's being holy that he is therefore remote, isolated, alien, inaccessible, distanced, separated, or estranged from our world of the ordinary. Modern critics are just plain uninformed when they accuse the Old Testament God of being such. No, the word *qodesh,* in and of itself, speaks of "holiness in our midst," "holiness making contact with us," "the different which is most conspicuous because of its contrast to the ordinary within which it appears."

This "involvement" belonging to *qodesh* is germane rather than incidental to its character. God's holiness is not so much a characterization of what he happens *to be,* of who he is in himself, as it is a description of his *function,* his action toward us (i.e., toward the whole mundane world). God's holiness is a purposeful activity. It is deliberately *contagious.* That is to say, God wants to rub his holiness against our ordinariness precisely that the ordinary might thereby become "hallowed" (which word, always remember, is a form of the word "holy"). So, quite the contrary of "distance," "intimate contact" must be the essential implication of *qodesh* if the term is to carry its biblical meaning at all.

The prophet's call in the temple (Isaiah 6) is probably the Bible's most helpful commentary on *qodesh.* Although Uzziah — Isaiah's earthly ruler at the time — was a comparatively "good" king, the fact that he had contracted leprosy was seen as proof that, rather than *qodesh,* his essential character was that of uncleanness and unholiness. And as is the king, so is the nation he heads and represents.

In despair over this human condition, Isaiah, in the temple, is confronted now by Israel's true King, the God of *qodesh* — who this prophet regularly denominates "the Holy One of Israel" (which could even be read, "The One Who Hallows Israel"). But upon meeting this Holy One, the prophet's first, correct, and inevitable reaction is the deference: "I am an unclean individual out of an unclean people headed by a leprous king; for my eyes have now seen the differentness of Israel's true King." Until one gets an impression of what is truly "right," he cannot perceive how completely "wrong" is the situation in which he has been totally immersed. (Because leprosy was thought to be communicated as "bad breath," Isaiah's reference to "unclean *lips*" undoubtedly is meant to be read, "I am a moral leper out of a leprous people represented by a leprous king," and perhaps is meant further to suggest that a "prophet"—a spokesman for God—above all people, must have "clean lips.")

This confession (after the very pattern of our previous chapter's "exhomologesis") is right to the point. It does not stick upon the negative side of exhomologesis, implying that people must be forced to admit they are sinners before God will have anything to do with them. Quite the contrary, it is precisely Isaiah's encountering the thrice-holy King (with the attendant implications of positive exhomologesis) that makes the prophet ready, willing, and even happy to confess his own uncleanness—and that certainly not as *worse than* but as *part of* the total uncleanness of humanity. This is how negative-positive exhomologesis is meant to operate. And it proves to be the one condition necessary for God's *qodesh* to go to work.

In a contact symbolized in the coals taken from the altar, God's *qodesh* hallows Isaiah—purging him, cleansing him, forgiving him—to the point that he becomes qualified (and only thus becomes sufficiently clean-lipped) to serve as a prophet of this holy God. The entire incident is a graphic demonstration of what *qodesh* is, how it operates, and what it is intent to accomplish. (And the point of the sermon is not—as it so often gets preached among us—Isaiah's heroic volunteering to be God's prophet but the incomparable *qodesh* of God that can make a prophet out of even a leper.)

However, in itself, the word *qodesh* originally did not tell us the *nature* of God's "difference," did not specify in what, explicitly, lies the distinction between God and the mundane. Nevertheless, Hebrew thought soon felt the need of filling that gap and so, in effect, shaded *qodesh* over into the package of words we shall next examine.

God as JUDGE

(infrequently *dayyan* [dah-yahn']
from the verb *din* [deen], "to discern";
regularly *shaphat* [shah-fat'],
both the noun "a magistrate"
and the verb "to act as a magistrate")

Here is the center point of our study. When scripture proceeds to specify in what way God's *qodesh* shows up as most conspicuously different from mundane normality, the answer invariably concerns justice and righteousness. In short, the main distinction between God and man is an *ethical* one. It is not primarily a matter of ontology (that God's "being" is different, that we are flesh and he is spirit). It is not primarily a matter of power, or of control over, or of rank, or of status. It is a matter of *ethics.* Thus, our English translation does accurately preserve the implication the Hebrew term picked up. For us to call God "holy" is as much as synonymous with calling him "righteous," or "good."

So, from the Garden and right on through (in fact he was authoritatively pronouncing things good even a chapter ahead of the Garden), God's is preeminently an ethical authority, one that distinguishes right from wrong, good from evil. The Bible consistently stresses (as with the "leprosy" of Isaiah 6) that it is precisely here we most need God's holiness and here where it is most essential that we defer to him. Then recall that it is also precisely here Adam wanted the fruit of the tree of the knowledge of good and evil (i.e., his own, independent, self-controlled source of such knowledge) so he wouldn't have to defer to God in these matters. And finally, it is precisely here modern man most staunchly refuses to defer: "There ain't nobody going to say what's right *for me; that's* my own prerogative!"

When we want to talk about God in this primary role as authority on matters of good and evil ("*He* has showed you, O man, what is good," as the neglected line of Micah 6:8 has it), the best metaphor for the job is to call him "Judge." On the human level, an authority on matters of good and evil is precisely what a judge is (or is supposed to be)—and that particularly so according to the Hebrew, biblical understanding. To call God "holy" almost inevitably leads to calling him "Judge"—and in a bit we shall discover that Isaiah's going, rather, from "holy" to "king" does not contradict the observation at all.

As shall become apparent, the Old Testament much more often uses *shaphat* as a verb describing God's "judging" than as a noun identifying him as "the judge." Yet, in both cases, it is the same word—and a very big one, too. For one thing, the biblical usage will force us to correct our picture of a judge. We will see that God does not appear primarily as a figure feared because of the condemnation and punishment he represents. Much more often he is welcomed as the one hope that human wrongness ever get straightened out and set right. Indeed, what this world most needs is a Judge.

Although it is not a technical term whose Hebrew we need to learn, there is another title for God that goes right along with and gives added emphasis to "Judge." Surprisingly enough, it is "King." Our own experience with kings is remote enough that we forget that, in biblical times, a king was not only the Supreme Court of his nation but also head of the whole judicial system. Biblically, of course, kings are also commanders of the armies (defenders of land) and administrators of government. However, if we were to analyze how the Bible uses the word "king" and what it has to say about kings, it might well turn out that they are most often seen as "agents of justice and righteousness." Not every reference, of course, but a great many of them speak either of the divine king or of human kings in just this way. So, along with "Judge," this study should help us correct, upgrade, and rehabilitate the biblical concept of God as "King."

There are, then, a couple more very important Hebrew terms that are part of our justice-and-righteousness package, essential in filling out its depth and significance.

The first is *mishpat* [mish-paht'], the judgment (sentence, decree, decision, law, or whatever) handed down by a judge. Etymologically, *mishpat* is derived from the same root as *shaphat*. In meaning, *mishpat* is closely related to *torah* (teaching, instruction, law) — although *mishpat* is the more strictly juridical term. Yet, *mishpat* is also a very big and important word in the Old Testament. As it might be put: A *shaphat* does his *shaphat* by rendering *mishpat,* which itself creates the situation of *tsedeq* (i.e., a judge does his judging by rendering judgment, or justice, which itself makes the situation right, or righteous). Yet, the all-important consideration is that humanity receive true and authoritative *mishpat.* There is no other hope that things ever can come right.

The second term, then, is *tsedeq/tsedaqah* [tseh'-dek/ tsed-ah-kah'] which can be translated "right, righteousness, to make right" — or just as properly, "just, justice, to justify." *Tsedeq* and *tsedaqah* are simply the masculine and feminine forms of the same word (but without any sort of gender implication); there is neither any difference in meaning nor any rule as to which is to be used when.

The "justice" translations probably speak more directly to the modern ear. However, the "right" translations may be helpful in keeping us reminded that *tsedeq* signifies far more than simply our modern liberal democratic definition of "justice." For instance, our Pledge of Allegiance, with its "liberty and *justice* for all," doesn't begin to intend the same thing as Old Testament *tsedeq*. For one thing *tsedeq* is always a "religious" term before it is a "political-ethical" one; it regularly includes a reference to God. Essentially, it denotes that will of God which is to be done on earth as it is in heaven, that which God has in mind for his people, his community, his world. Consequently, only when the word goes on to specify what it is, in particular, that God wants—only then does *tsedeq* come to denote goodness, righteousness, justice, and the correction of all things.

Yet, even in this, *tsedeq* does not settle for our western understanding of "justice" with its "to each as he deserves—equal rights, opportunities, et al." *Tsedeq* pushes, rather, toward the principle, "to each according to his *need*," thus going far beyond simple "justice" to something more like "grace." And in the Old Testament, *tsedeq* is a very big word indeed. It may even be the most crucial of the lot, identifying, as it does, the special *content* of God's judgment rather than merely its *form*.

However, *tsedeq* manages to get even bigger as the Old Testament goes along. By the time we get into the second part of Isaiah (if not before), the word has grown even beyond any ethical reference to mean "victory," vindication," "salvation." The move has logic behind it: when God accomplishes his will *(tsedeq)* by infusing the life of the world with his righteousness *(tsedeq)*, that *is* victory, vindication, and salvation *(tsedeq)*. In order to cover the richness of the word *tsedeq*, biblical translators are forced to use several different English words to translate it in its different contexts. Consequently, we easily can lose track of the fact that we are dealing with just one biblical concept. Thus, in the study to follow, the King James Version has some advantage, because—although it may read awkwardly—it does a good job of preserving the identity of the word *tsedeq*.

Regarding our package as a whole, then, notice first that all of these Hebrew words have direct reference to God and will not perform correctly apart from that reference. They are not used as we use them in English, as secular words we are free to give religious meaning only if and when we choose to. Thus, as we have suggested, *tsedeq* is never simply what we might choose to call "justice"; it is "God's justice," something quite different. Notice, secondly, that all the way through this line of thought the terminology has stayed within the metaphor of God as "Judge." This chapter (with the previous one) should convince us as to how central the concept actually is in biblical thought.

Confession, *yadah* [yah-dah']

Most of the above sequence comes from Snaith. This final element does not. In our previous chapter, we saw how Markus Barth brings out the comparable New-Testament/Pauline string at a somewhat different place. The above, of course, all speaks of God's initiative and authority. But what, then, does the Old Testament see as the appropriate human response to all this Judge-judgment-justification business? We here have been calling it "deference." Barth suggested that Paul calls it *exhomologesis* ("confession"). But the closest Old Testament Hebrew equivalent to Paul's Greek is apparently *yadah* (confession, praise, adoration, worship). Wherever the King James Version of the Old Testament has "confess" or "confession," the original Hebrew had *yadah* or a closely related word. However, about half the places where the English Old Testament has "praise," the Hebrew was still *yadah*. The Hebrew *yadah* apparently is a bit more flexible than the Greek *exhomologesis*. Yet, in the study to follow, it will become plain that Paul was saying nothing new but simply giving a Greek voice to the ancient Hebrew faith.

The Justice Package in the Old Testament

From this point, you will need a Bible to use alongside my text. I will cite much more scripture than can be reprinted here. Be clear, however, that I am not apologizing for the fact that my book requires a supplement. In actuality, it is that supplement that may make my book worthwhile.

In preparing this study, I simply went to Young's Concordance to locate the Old Testament occurrences of the technical "judge terms": *din, shaphat, mishpat, tsedeq*. Related words become involved only by virtue of their natural association with these. Out of Young's list of countless occurrences (at least more than I chose to count) I have selected only those of particular theological significance. My first thought was to arrange them into some sort of logical order or outline. However, the different ideas are so completely intertwined that it proves wiser to handle them simply in the order they appear in the Bible itself.

Genesis 18:25 & 19. We touched upon verse 25 in the previous chapter as an invitation to *exhomologesis* (which has now become *yadah)*. Now, looking at it in Hebrew, it reads: "Shall not the *Shaphat* of all the earth do *mishpat?*" And in verse 19, Abraham is "to keep the way of the Lord by doing *mishpat* and *tesedaqah"* and so receive what God has promised him.

If I read correctly, "Judge," here in 18:25, is the very first metaphor (or metaphoric title) scripture ascribes to God. Up to this point he has been called simply "God." English translations have used "Lord" only to represent the Hebrew name "Yahweh." And he has been called "God Most High" and "God Almighty." But none of these are metaphorical personifications describing God in terms of human analogy.

The occurrence here, of course, does not prove that, in point of time, "Judge" was the very first metaphor ever applied to God. It can, however, be taken as a symbol of *theological* priority. The remainder of our study seems to indicate that "Judge" is far and away the one most central metaphor by which the Bible understands God—this to the point it is safe to say that any modern concept of God which cannot support these "judging attributes" will not serve as the "God" of the biblical message or the Christian faith. Thus, "God" as "the Ground of Being" "Creative Process," "Sympathetic Companion" (who is allowed to express only acceptance and understanding but never authoritative judgment), "World Spirit"—anything less than or exclusive of "Judge"—simply will not pass the muster of our rule of faith and practice.

And it can hardly be accidental that verse 19 stands this close to verse 25. It strengthens our case by identifying "the way of the Lord" as the doing of *mishpat* and *tsedeqah,* which in turn will lead to promised salvation. It is very important to observe the sequence and priority within this verse. It definitely is not said that, if only you will pursue your implicit understanding (or your culturally determined concept) of "justice and righteousness," the very doing so will, in effect, have you upon "the way of the Lord." No, just the other way around, this verse tells us to go to the Lord, get with him, follow him, learn from him, and be enabled by him . . . then you will discover that you *are* promoting what *he* defines as "justice and righteousness." If we may put it so, scripture makes conversion a prerequisite of doing justice.

Genesis 30:1-6. Rachel has been scorned and put down for being barren. But now that she has given her husband a son through her maidservant, she celebrates this as God's vindicating *judgment* of her case and calls the child "Dan" (obviously from the *din* root, "to judge"). Rachel's glory lies in the fact that she has been judged of God; and her reference to God's judgment comes within a doxology (a word of praise to God). And wonder of wonders, this will prove to be standard practice within the Old Testament. It is precisely as "Judge" that God is most welcomed, worshipped, and praised. Obviously, in our turn, we moderns need to make a major adjustment in our understanding of God, in our worship and praise of him.

That the Old Testament Law is *torah* has the effect of bringing it at least close to our package. In human analogy, who would be the appropriate figure for the giving of *torah?* So the books of the Law (Exodus, Leviticus, Numbers, and Deuteronomy) do also see their legislation—whether that of personal morality, social justice, or ritual procedure—as being decrees *(mishpat)* of God the Judge. A few select verses will establish the orientation.

Leviticus 18:4-5. The *torah* represents God's *mishpat* (ordinances) and not simply Israel's own cultural tradition. Also, this *mishpat* is seen as the way to "life" rather than as a repressive code and an excuse for punishment.

Deuteronomy 1:16-17. At base, all judgment—even that mediated through human judges—is to be God's and not man's. And being God's, its prime characteristic is that it be entirely impartial, taking pains to hear the small as well as the great—including even "aliens."

Deuteronomy 32:4 & 36. Here again we have confession within the context of worship. God is praised explicitly as Judge. In verse 36, the Judge is seen as Savior. That the Lord will judge *(din)* his people is actually translated "vindicate" in some versions. And notice, again, the distinct bias in favor of down-and-outers.

Judges 11:27. It is neither that might makes right nor even that human judgment makes right. God is the Judge whose decree ultimately decides even international, historical disputes.

1 Samuel 2:1-10. As earlier with Rachel, here Hannah's doxology praises the Lord for the gift of a child, in the process portraying God primarily as Judge. (We are onto a pattern that would include Mary's Magnificat, if we were to go into the New Testament.) In verse 2 and following, God's "holiness" transmutes directly into the ethical activity of "judging"; and God's "judgment" becomes the equivalent of "vindication and salvation" — with the customary bias in favor of the poor and lowly. In verse 10, then, God's activity is explicitly called "judging"; and there is probably the implication that the making of this sort of righteous judgment is also the primary function of the human "king."

1 Samuel 8:5-6. The Israelites, of course, are dead wrong in wanting a human king in place of God's kingship. However, they are altogether right in their understanding of what a king should be. The RSV says that they wanted a king to "govern" them; but the Hebrew word is *shaphat*. We need to catch up to these primitive and wrongheaded Israelites in welcoming and seeking out "judgment" as the one hope of ever getting things right.

1 Kings 3:28. The king, Solomon, has his motion seconded for properly playing the role of "judge" when two women claimed the one baby. That is what kings are supposed to be — and how we are to respond.

2 Chronicles 19:5-7. Very specifically, human judges are to act as deputies of Judge Jehovah and show the same qualities.

Proverbs 29:14 & 31:9. The central duty of a king is to be a true judge, favoring the poor and needy.

Who would have guessed? But the one book of the Old Testament by far the richest in emphasis and insight regarding our justice package is PSALMS. Psalms, of course, is *worship* material. So here we are as much as told that worship *(yadah/exhomologesis)* is the proper context from which to approach justice and righteousness. To a great degree, worship must *consist* in praising God as Judge, as the source of and authority for all true justice. And this strange (to us) combination consequently catches two major sectors of the modern church. Those people who are strong on "worship" but weak or uninterested regarding "justice" are wrong. Even their emphatic "praising of the Lord" is defective for failing to credit God in his central role as Judge. But on the other hand, those people who are strong on "justice" but weak or uninterested in looking to God in the deference of "worship" are also wrong. Even their commitment to "justice" is defective for failing to be rooted in or defined from its true authority in Judge Jehovah. It could be that Psalms (of all books) carries the message most needed by the church of our day.

Psalm 7:1-11. In the judgment of God lies our only hope. Whether that judgment proves our condemnation or our vindication (or most likely both at once), it is the one way to salvation.

Psalm 9. This hymn of praise centers solely upon God as Judge. God's judgment is especially the hope of the poor and oppressed (vss. 9 & 18). But if getting a person's situation "justified" implies his coming into right relationship to the Judge even before it signifies the Judge's correcting of his outward circumstances, then our helping people to come to God (evangelism) should be considered "a doing of justice" that is just as valid and perhaps even more important than our raising their standard of living or doing anything else for them. In particular, human "justice" dare never displace God's justice (vss. 19-20).

Psalms 26:1; 35:24; 43:1. In each of these instances the worshipper prays that God will work his judgment *(shaphat)* upon the worshipper himself, confident that that Judge works in all things for good. This must strike us as a rather new idea: volunteering for judgment instead of trying to evade it. (By the way, there, as well as throughout Psalms and the scriptures as a whole, we should be ready to read confession, prayer, and praise both as the voice of the individual believer and of the faith community. God is Judge in both relationships, and we need him in both. His judgment is as necessary for our individual lives [personal righteousness] as for the life of society [social justice]—and the Bible always plays it both ways. However, when anyone regularly calls for God's judgment upon the outside world—church, state, or culture—but never upon himself, we do right to be suspicious.)

Psalm 50. This is an explicit courtroom scene in which God appears as Judge over the whole creation. Verse 23 makes it clear that the deference of worship is the proper response to the Judge, that justice/justification is a matter of getting right with him (being made right by him) even before it is a matter of ethical behavior, and that being judged by God is the one way to salvation.

Psalm 51:1-17. The dominant theme is doxology and confession. The subject of that worship is God the Judge. Mercy, love, forgiveness, cleansing, and grace are seen as components of his "judgment" rather than being the different or contrary actions of a different figure. Even if God's true judgment must be that I am a sinner, I still want it to happen, knowing it is only through such judgment the situation can be changed.

Psalm 72:1-7, 12-14. This is a royal psalm in which prayer is made for the earthly monarch. Yet it also is explicitly stated that his central role is as the agent of God's justice—even to a special responsibility for the poor. Verse 7 suggests (rightly) that "peace" is an essential component of the justice and righteousness package.

Psalm 75:1-3. Doxology again is emphatic. Also, it is observed that only God's action as Judge has kept the world from going to smash long before this. (So how dare we suggest that only our efforts can save it now?)

Psalm 76:1-9. God's judgment means peace (vs. 3), victory (vss. 5-6), and salvation (vs. 9).

Psalm 89:14-18. Here we find practically our whole package in five verses, one line after another: (1) the biggies of "righteousness and justice"; (2) with which "steadfast love *(hesed)* and faithfulness" rightfully belong; (3) doxology and exhomologesis; (4) God's judging as part of his being "King"; and (5) all of this signifying his holiness *(qodesh)*.

Psalm 96. Nowhere is there be found any greater expression of doxology and praise. And for what is God praised? See verses 10 & 13.

Psalm 98. Here God is praised for the victory (vss. 1-3), that makes him King (vs. 6), but which is all a result of his being Judge (vs. 9).

Psalm 99:1-5. God carries authority as Lord (vss. 1-2), which is his holiness (vss. 3 & 5), that of a Mighty King (vs. 4), whose primary character is that he is a lover and executor of justice (vs. 4).

Psalm 103:1-14. We are to bless the Lord and hallow his name (vs. 1) and forget not all his benefits (vs. 2) — which include forgiveness and healing (vs. 3), redemption, love, and mercy (vs. 4), the giving of all good things (vs. 5), and much more of the same (vss. 7-14). Yet, all of this is to be understood as the action of a Judge rather than anyone else (vss. 6 & 10).

The *prophets* of the Old Testament, of course, are known for their emphasis on "justice and righteousness." Yet, our study has already made it apparent that they were merely carriers and developers of the tradition. They certainly did not found it or have a corner on this theology. Among the prophets, the book of Isaiah (in all its parts) is easily the one that is strongest and most creative in this regard (partly, perhaps, because it is a much bigger book than many). So we will now center on that book and pick up only a few supplementary insights from others of the prophets.

Isaiah 1:21-27. Much more than upon merely our social-ethical behavior, "justice" depends upon our faithfulness to the Judge. It is *because* she became a harlot in relationship to him that the city lost her righteousness (vs. 21). And that Zion is to be redeemed by justice (vs. 27) does not denote a works-righteousness which says that, if Zion will make herself good by practicing justice, God will accept her back as redeemed. No, quite the reverse, it will be the Judge's gracious justifying of her that will again make her capable of living justly.

Isaiah 2:2-5. We customarily have valued this passage for its promise of "peace." But we have largely missed the point that this peace is created directly as a work of the Judge (vss. 3-4a). Our peace witness would be stronger and more biblical if we were to keep it in the context Isaiah gives it. We ought not think we can create the political reality of peace while ignoring the religious move of coming to God for judgment and justification.

Isaiah 3:13-15. This is a judgment scene of the sort found frequently in the writings of the prophets.

Isaiah 4:2-5. Even though painful (as "a spirit of burning"), it is good and necessary for us to be hallowed through God's judgment. The outcome is a closeness to God and a leading by him such as Israel experienced in the Exodus.

Isaiah 5:16. Isaiah is the biblical writer strongest on God's holiness. Here he as much as equates *qodesh* and *tsedeq*. Specifically, it is as Judge that God is holy.

Isaiah 9:2-7. Notice, once, that this so familiar passage applies to the *Messiah* the very package of terms we have seen attributed to God as Judge: (a) doxology and praise (vs. 3); (b) victory (vss. 4-5); (c) kingship (vss. 6-7); (d) peace (vss. 6-7); (e) the establishment of justice and righteousness (vs. 7); and (f) the fact that God is the doer of it all (vs. 7). Old Testament messianic prophecy (and thus Jesus himself) belongs squarely within our theology of justice.

Isaiah 11:1-9. This is another of Isaiah's great messianic passages. This one, again, culminates in a vision of worldwide peace (vss. 6-9). Here it is made very explicit that the kingly Messiah is essentially a judge (vss. 3b-5). It is curious how we have so completely overlooked the heart of the matter.

Isaiah 30:18. *Because* the Lord is a God of *mishpat,* he is also gracious and merciful. God's "judgment" is of a piece with these kindly qualities, not something different from them.

Isaiah 32:1, 16-17. Whether messianic or not (the matter is debated), this passage makes clear the king's role regarding justice (vs. 1) and the fact that such justice is the way of salvation that eventuates in peace (vss. 16-17).

Isaiah 33:2-6, 22. Judge Jehovah is victor and savior and "the stability of your times"—a phrase our "times" might well ponder (vss. 2-6). Judge = Ruler = King = Savior (vs. 22). All four of these titles must be understood as compatible not only with each other but with all we know of God. We have no grounds for resisting, dropping, or altering any of them.

With Chapter 40 begins the portion of the book often identified as Second or Deutero-Isaiah.

Isaiah 40:13-14. When, concerning God, the rhetorical question is asked, "Who taught him the path of *mishpat?*" the implication is that he is much more than simply one who knows justice and acts justly. He *invented* these ideas; and they are not to be found outside of or defined apart from him.

Isaiah 41:1-?. It is hard to say how far it runs; but Chapter 41 introduces the most extensive and detailed courtroom scene of the Bible.

Isaiah 42:1-4. Probably as a participant in that continuing courtroom scene, the Servant here (who certainly is to be identified with Chapter 53's Suffering Servant—who, in turn, Christians understand as pointing strongly to Jesus) is introduced explicitly as a justifying judge. Notice especially the possibility now presented that justice can be established through quietness and nonresistance rather than always the bluster and push so customary among us. "Political action" is not the only way to "justice"; and "justice" is a bigger concept than simply "that which is produced by political action." Yet, now we have seen that both Isaiah's Messiah-figure and Deutero's Servant-figure stand within our theology of justice. In the New Testament, it is particularly (though by no means exclusively) the Gospel of John that relates the judgment theme to Jesus. Yet, we seldom, if ever, consider him in such a context at all.

Isaiah 45:20-25. Here is the full-fledged trial scene we examined in our foregoing chapter — with its explicit identification of the Judge as World Savior and his guaranteeing a work of judgment that will compel universal *exhomologesis* and *yadah*.

Isaiah 51:4-6. The world Judge is to be world Savior; and it is through his justifying action that salvation takes place.

Isaiah 53:11. Who is the Suffering Servant and what does he accomplish? In his death, he, the just *(tsaddiq)* Servant, justifies *(tsadaq)* the many. As earlier we saw that it is through contact with God's "holiness" we are "hallowed," so now we see that it is through contact with the "justice" of the self-giving Servant we are "justified." Deutero is with Paul and Markus Barth in seeing Jesus' death-and-resurrection as a juridical action that establishes justice. Although the concept "justice" cannot here be said to cancel any of its political-ethical implications, it does certainly push far beyond them.

From this point, our references are to the third part of Isaiah.

Isaiah 56:1. Keeping justice and doing righteousness are the means by which we make ourselves ready for salvation; the New Testament might say "anticipate the kingdom of God."

Isaiah 59:7-20. This passage forms a beautiful conclusion to our study of Isaiah and gives us the word we perhaps most need to hear. Neither peace, justice, righteousness, nor truth is to be found in us or in any of our ways; our ways are rather those of sin, iniquity, and unfaithfulness (vss. 7-15a). It is only when the Lord decides he has had as much as he can take that he will rouse himself in the judgment that signifies redemption's victory (vss. 15b-20).

The other prophets are in essential agreement with the Isaianic tradition; so from them we take only a few particularly striking references.

Jeremiah 9:23-24. Although we tend to see them as quite distinct, steadfast love *(hesed)* here is coupled directly with justice and righteousness as the things in which the Lord delights.

Jeremiah 22:15-16. In God's eyes, it was precisely Josiah's righteous judging (particularly toward the poor and needy) that had made him a true king and proved that he "knew" the Lord.

Jeremiah 23:5-6. The hallmark of the day of the Messiah (what the New Testament knows as Jesus' coming with the kingdom of God) is that justice will be complete. And the name by which the Messiah will be called is: "Yahweh is our *tsedeq.*" It definitely is not a case of our coming full of good works and saying, "These dedicated efforts are our righteousness." No, the Judge himself is our righteousness.

Hosea 12:6. Love and justice rightly are coupled. The RSV and NEB translations tell us that God's is the very power that turns us toward these ideals—so that moving to God himself is the only proper way of getting to them. These qualities have no reality apart from him.

Amos 5:24. Amos' famous verse undoubtedly intends, not that we create "justice" according to our own ideas of what it should be, but that we get out of the way and let God's justice roll down as it is meant to do and wants to do.

Micah 3:1 & 8. Our earlier chapter on 6:8 showed how closely Micah relates justice and worship. In review, here, in verse 1, the prophet insists that it is of first importance for us to "know *mishpat.*" In verse 8, he claims that he knows *mishpat* and that such knowledge came to him (and presumably can come to anyone) only through "the Spirit of the Lord." Worship God and so learn justice from him—there is no other teacher.

Zechariah 7:9-10. Our "justice" should consist in rendering true judgments *but also* in showing kindness and mercy, doing deeds of service, not devising evil against anyone. Biblically, "justice" includes "grace" as well as what our political tradition calls "justice."

Zechariah 8:16-17. Again justice is broadened out far beyond mere social equity.

Deference, Worship, Exhomologesis, Yadah

We proposed at the outset that the proper response to authority is *deference.* Especially in the Psalms but also elsewhere in the Old Testament we have seen that, in relation to God the Judge, this deference is to take the form of joyful *worship.* In our previous chapter, we saw that Paul particularizes this worship as being negative-positive confession, *exhomologesis.* We discovered, then, that the Hebrew equivalent of exhomologesis is *yadah.* And that turns out to be one funny word.

Yadah is built upon the Hebrew root that means 'hand" and itself means literally "to use the hands." Now who but Jews would ever have come up with the idea that worshipping and praising God is something you do with your *hands?* Knees bow and tongues confess; but hands? The word apparently refers to the Jewish motion of throwing high one's hands in prayer and joy and praise.

So, in our day, it is the charismatics who preserve true worship, doing it by hand, hands up? Well, yes and no. Yes—as long as the accompanying song is: "He is Lord; he is Lord. He is risen from the dead, and he is Lord. Every knee shall bow, every tongue *confess,* that Jesus Christ is Lord!" You can't do any better than that!

But no—too much of the time the mood is all wrong. When the hands are up while singing "Hallelujah" to the most lugubrious lullaby ever composed, the motion says something different. Put the charismatic Hallelujah Song up against Handel's Hallelujah Chorus, and you will hear what I mean. The two betray completely opposite moods and spirits. Expressive of that difference, notice that Handel's "hallelujahs" lead on to "And HE shall reign forever and ever. King of kings and Lord of lords, forever." You can't do any better than that!

But too often the charismatic "hallelujahs" lead on to "Fill *my* cup, Lord. *I* lift it up, Lord. Come and quench this thirsting of *my* soul. Bread of heaven, feed *me* till *I* want no more. Fill *my* cup; fill it up; and make *me* whole." Surely we can do a lot better than that! Much of the time, I am afraid, the charismatic lifted hands represent a desire to take to ourselves blessings *from* God rather than our bestowing blessing upon his name—confessing and exalting him sheerly for who he is.

However, let me be quick to say that I don't know of any other sector of the church doing a better job of *yadah*. The charismatics are at least getting their hands toward God instead of sitting on them — as is the case when worship becomes "a celebration of our humanity," or an opportunity to share our feelings or do analyses of the human condition. In all this, our tendency is to recognize and value God only to the extent he is found useful to and affirmative of our program of human development and self-actualization.

But no, go again to the Psalms and see that only the motion of forgetting self and throwing everything toward him qualifies as *yadah*. "Shall not the Judge of all the earth do right?" *Yadah;* get 'em up there! For, it is clear, this is the only human action that can get us into the theology of *justice*.

CHAPTER EIGHT

Barth and the Brethren

Another chapter, another Barth. Chapter 6, son Markus, *ex-homologesis* [13 letters]. Chapter 8, father Karl, *mythologoumenon* [15 letters]. I isn't going to be easy to beat out the old man!

From Infamous Indianapolis I went directly to Peaceful Pennsylvania and from listening to Brethren to reading Barth. "Oh, what a relief it is!" The book was Karl Barth's newly published *The Christian Life* [Eerdmans], the last segment of his epic *Church Dogmatics* to be even partially completed before his death in 1968. It was like going from one theological world into another. And some of Barth's observations are so appropriate that they simply demand inclusion here.

However, I want first to use the occasion as an opening for some observations regarding the Brethren and theologians in general. Karl Barth was undoubtedly the most renowned and respected Christian theologian of the present century—and perhaps even back to the days of Luther and Calvin. This is not to say he should be treated as though he were infallible or anything of the sort. It is to say he deserves higher regard than Brethren generally are inclined to give to him or to any other theologians.

Unfortunately, among us, not even the clergy (let alone the laity) show much interest in theology. In the face of a theological statement that fails to suit our fancy, the response tends to be, "Well, that's one person's opinion"—with nary a thought that it may in actuality be the product of a careful study of Christian tradition and thus the consensus of the long-term, ever-so-broad faith community. The Brethren preference (if theology there must be) is rather to find someone called a "theologian" whose ideas we like; then we latch onto him. In doing so, we ignore the fact that our Brethrenism commits us to the New Testament's being our rule of faith. We act as though there are no criteria for distinguishing good from bad, true from false theology — as though any theologian in print has just as much chance of being right as any other.

Or what is worse, we make the witless assumption that *our own* theological ideas have just as much validity as do those of, say, Karl Barth. Consequently, we treat his lifetime of reading and study — let alone his eminent intellectual gifts — as carrying no weight at all. We acknowledge the expertise of auto mechanics in their field far above that of theologians in theirs.

But what must be borne in mind is that the heart of Brethrenism (or that of any other denomination) is not a blank which you are invited to fill in according to your own whim. Neither is the name of any particular theology or theologian (even Karl Barth) to appear there. No, there, we have seen, stands the line: The New Testament is our rule of faith and practice.

Now we should be quick to note that not every "theologian" even claims to accept this Brethren premise. Many choose, rather, to make their theology conform to the world of modern thought, to what best suits the mentality of the age. There is no particular mystery or secret about this. Bible scholars and the theological community itself would generally agree as to which thinkers are more biblically oriented and which less. In many cases, the theologian himself would be ready to admit which is his authority. For instance, Karl Barth did biblical theology and Paul Tillich, philosophical — no problem. Yet, our "heart commitment" does not leave us Brethren free to play the field. In seeking theological help, we are obligated at least to look first in the direction of *biblical* theology.

Among recognized theologians of our day, Karl Barth has been the one most noted for his command of the Bible, the one most knowledgeable about the Christian tradition that has conserved and interpreted the faith through the centuries. Further, he was strongly committed to keeping his own thought and teaching within these parameters. Of course, none of this is to say that the Church of the Brethren is under obligation to be in agreement with

Karl Barth at every point. It does say what cannot be said regarding just every theologian, namely, that we share with him this commitment to a common, New Testament center.

So we are not bound to accept any of the following presentation simply because Karl Barth said it. Always we must ask whether Barth is being biblically accurate—and that not simply in the sense of whether he can support his ideas by quoting scripture (which he does, at length) but whether his thought does itself replicate the major themes and patterns of the Bible.

In this connection, let me be on record that I do not consider myself a biblical scholar and so nowhere in this book mean to be rendering any authoritative, technical judgments. However, I have done enough teaching and reading in the field to know who the biblical authorities are and where they stand. And I can say without fear of contradiction that, among the generality of scholars who know the Bible best, the two father-and-son pairs we have used, Blumhardt and Barth, are highly respected as being entirely reliable interpreters of scripture (as are the not-father-and-son pair of Lutherans, Kierkegaard and Bonhoeffer—plus freelancers like Hengel and Snaith). You would have a hard time finding anyone better qualified than this crew.

In this particular volume of his *Church Dogmatics,* Barth is dealing with the nature of the Christian life, what he calls "ethics." We must, however, give some attention to what he means by that term, because his treatment is the farthest thing from what usually appears under the name. Customarily, "ethics" is the last area of Christian thought to be biblically oriented—most often taking its start from where the Bible leaves off. Barth, on the other hand, is talking about the *theological* stance (i.e., the nature of the relationship to God) which he understands to be the prerequisite of Christian *ethics*. He does this through the unheard of ploy of expounding the Lord's Prayer. ("Why should anyone go to the Lord's Prayer to do *ethics*, for crying out loud?") Although Barth does not recognize the fact, what he actually is doing is picking up the theme Micah introduced in our earlier chapter, namely, the insistence that "worship" and "justice" cannot be separated, that true worship—

which, of course, is what the Lord's Prayer is — is the only way to true ethics. As we said, Barth is nothing if not biblical.

In his exposition, Barth centers in on the Brethren (likely without even knowing that there is such a church) under his treatment of the first petition, "Hallowed be thy name." He points out that, because this is a *petition,* it clearly assumes that, neither previously nor presently, have we been properly hallowing God's name; you don't pray to be given what you already have. Likewise, the petition must also assume that, on our own, we are not even *capable* of hallowing God's name — else we could simply proceed instead of calling upon him to do it for himself. So this is a prayer that God himself act to put an end to the desecration and dishonoring of his name which we are powerless to stop, if not actually being party to its continuance. Although again he doesn't say so, Barth is effectually recognizing the negative-positive combination of *exhomologesis:* "We confess that we are not for much as 'hallowers' — being too busy in trying to get our own names hallowed (which ain't easy) — but we must also acknowledge that your name is truly holy and is the one name worthy of being hallowed among us."

Barth recognizes that Christians — as others — are motivated by a whole host of passions, some good and some not so good. However, paramount for the Christian should be a burning zeal for the honor of God, a driving concern that he receive the glory due him. "Hallowed be *thy* name!" If, then, as with so many Christians of our day, the priority of your life is that injustices be made right, consider that the greatest injustice ever perpetrated is our refusal to credit God for his justice, for the wonder of all he has given and accomplished in behalf of humanity. Indeed, God's concern that his name be hallowed certainly is not for the sake of any ego need on his part. It — as with everything of God — is for *our* sake. Until we can see the rightness of glorifying him, we obviously have no true understanding of "rightness" in any connection. If we can't catch on to how unjustly we have treated him, we have no idea of what injustice is. If, in worship, we are unable to recognize "justice" in the Just Judge and his action in the death and resurrection of Jesus Christ, there is little chance that we can recognize it anywhere. If we refuse to do justice to God in *worship,* we certainly will never do it for others in *ethics.* "Hallowed be thy name!"

Yet, it cannot be said that contemporary Brethrenism is marked by any particular zeal for the honor of God. ("It takes all of my time . . . to work at this world of peace, justice, and liberation we've got coming along.") This was demonstrated to me by careful observation of that Indianapolis Conference. In the preliminary song services, as we sang "the grand old hymns of the church," or as we read scripture, there was *exhomologesis* aplenty (there is no doubt about where our worship *used* to focus). However, as soon as the scene shifted to contemporary Brethren materials—hymns, litanies, prayers, and sermons—the focus shifted as well. Now there came to prominence a narcissistic fascination with "the human." The talk was all of our faith pilgrimages, our religious experience, our self-fulfillment, our liberation, our desire to feel good about ourselves. And even when things were not this self-centered, they still focused on the pathos of the human condition, humankind's dreams for the future, our getting the world into the shape we have in mind for it. It became evident that God there was recognized only insofar as he serves our human venture. It is for us to act and for him to affirm those actions. As I said, when, on the day following Conference, I started reading Barth, it spelled r-e-l-i-e-f.

Within Barth's section on "Hallowed Be Thy Name," he has a subsection entitled "The Known and Unknown God." That God is "known" has reference to the fact that he has acted powerfully in revealing (and even presenting) himself to the whole human world.

(1) He has made himself known through the church's work of proclamation, evangelism, and missions. It is true, of course, that we have not been as faithful in these endeavors as we should have been. It is true, too, that we often have distorted the picture of God in the process of painting it before the world. Nevertheless, it is the case that God has used (and used mightily) this means of making himself known.

(2) As the Apostle Paul tells us, God has also revealed himself in a way that any person could perceive if he chose to, namely, through the nature and life of the created order. This "natural theology" surely is not sufficient to bring one to an adequate

knowledge of God as Lord and Savior; but it does establish that it is a person's own sinful fault for not knowing any more of God than he does.

(3) The third way in which God has revealed himself is of an order entirely different from the other two, in that it is the only one in which a true, full, and perfect knowledge is truly, fully, and perfectly communicated (not perfectly *received* by us, obviously, yet perfectly communicated by God). This, of course, is God's revelation in Jesus Christ—his life, death, resurrection, exaltation, and coming again. Here God has made himself known in a way that cannot otherwise even be approached, let alone matched.

In calling God "unknown," Barth has reference to the ways in which we have managed to ignore, reject, and even pervert the "knowing him" God has offered through his self-revelations. God has made himself known; but by and large we prefer not to know him. Barth organizes this topic by speaking first of how the knowledge of God is refused in the *world* and then how it is refused in the *church*.

The knowledge of God is resisted in the world, first, through deliberate, self-conscious *atheism*. (Barth analyzes this phenomenon at some length.) Secondly, God-knowledge is resisted through *religion,* i.e., the human, cultural impulse to create belief systems. "In religion, [the world] tries to deal with him by establishing itself behind a wall of self-invented and self-made images of God, so that it may really be left to itself" [p. 130]. (Barth's treatment of God-resisting "religion" is too complex to even try to summarize here.)

Barth's third category is one particularly relevant to the Church of the Brethren. It is somewhat strange that he includes it under "world" when what he describes is much more obviously "church." I think he must have had in mind that this "churchliness" is actually only "worldliness in disguise."

There is, however, a desecration of the name of God which in comparison to that in atheism and that in the religions is even worse. This is the attempt of the world to exalt its own cause as God's or, conversely, to subject God's cause to its own, to make it serve it. . . . This attempt arises when the world, unavoidably confronted by God even though it does not know him, believes that he can be very useful and even indispensable to its own goals and aims and aspirations; so that, instead of denying him or coming to terms with him with a bit of religion, it takes the cleverer course of resolutely affirming him, affirming itself in and with him, affirming his deity as its own and its own as his. . . . Now it equates God with itself or itself with God. . . . It thinks it can be an infinitely better, more effective, and more triumphant world if it is with him instead of being against him or only incidentally and partially with him. It even thinks that it can really be happy and certain about what it wills and does in politics, economics, law, and society, in work and leisure, in culture and education, in science and art, if it can understand and do everything in the radiance and dignity of the slogan: God wills it! God does it! It thinks its freedom of control is really ensured if God is the world-God and itself the God-world, if it may be secular in its piety and pious in its secularity. . . . How there can be a transition from this to the knowledge of God, it is difficult and even impossible to see.

[pp. 130-31]

Let me put the matter as mildly and generously as I can: I invite you to consider whether the Church of the Brethren (or your own denomination) is not engaged in a dangerous flirtation with the very temptation Barth so graphically describes. And with that, we need to be quick to report what Barth himself is quick to say both at this point and at points following: None of these indictments is meant to suggest that either God, Barth, or we mean to consign such churches to damnation or advocate that they be abandoned or dissolved. Because, at every point, our faith is in *God* rather than in any sort of church entity, we can share Barth's firmly expressed confidence that no church (or individual) can drift beyond the possibility of God's getting it turned around, set right, forgiven, and redeemed. At least for Vernard Eller, let it be said that nothing in this book means that I have given up on the Church of the Brethren. The sickness is diagnosed as a step toward the patient's recovery, not as an excuse for deserting and rejecting him.

Regarding resistance against knowing God *in the church,* Barth then divides his analysis into "the church in *excess*" and "the church in *defect.*" What he only hints, I will make explicit, namely, that it is quite possible for one and the same church to be both excessive and defective simultaneously. But with "the church in excess," Barth has in mind denominations at the opposite end of the ecclesiological spectrum from the Church of the Brethren. He names the Roman Catholic Church and implies other high-church, formalized bodies of state-church background. Yet, particularly on the contemporary American scene, it seems that "low," believer churches are just as liable to their own excesses of pretension, image-building, and pop-cultural hype.

> The one form of the denial and apostasy is the church in excess, the presumptuous church which exalts itself and puffs itself up. . . . The church in excess is the church exceeding the limit within which it alone can be the church of Jesus Christ. . . . The threat is that it will serve its own needs instead of him, that it will become its own means of life and glory. . . . In whose honor is so much pomp put forth, for whom is there such energetic and skillful propaganda? . . . It becomes and is the church in excess by boasting about him in order to be able to boast about itself. . . . That [God] gives himself to it, the church takes to mean that he is in its hands. It will not be without reservation a creature of the Word (Luther), a church which simply and unequivocally serves him. Appealing to its insitution and empowering through him, it wants to be the church that reigns in his name.
>
> [pp. 136-37]

However, it is under "the church in defect" that Barth would seem to be zeroing in more directly upon the Church of the Brethren (he couldn't have *known* about us, could he?).

> The other form of apostasy is the church in defect, the church which does not take itself seriously enough because it is only half sure of its cáuse [namely, whether its is the cause of God or only of man]. . . . It is unfaithful because it neglects and denies . . . that its Lord—he is its determination—is the *living* Lord. . . . To be sure, it knows and recites the words: "The third day he rose again from the dead; he ascended into heaven, and sitteth on the right hand of God the Father Almighty." But it does not say this with total confidence, only with half confidence. It does not stand defiantly on it. . . . It is the church that certainly looks to Jesus Christ but not without the subsidiary thought that perhaps he is only an idea or a *mythologoumenon* [look it up for yourself; I've done my share with *exhomologesis;* but it appears to me that simply jamming together "mythological" and

"phenomenon" would come pretty close to the mark] to whom it might be dangerous to cling. It wants to go to him, to celebrate Christmas, Easter, and Pentecost seriously, to be the Christian church, but it finds and feels itself burdened by the fact that it is also powerfully impressed and frightened by the world around it. . . . The church in defect is the church which looks anxiously to its Lord but even more anxiously to everything else; which painfully compares itself to the world; which for this reason seeks possible points of contact from or to it; which is intent on bridges from the one place to the other. The favorite word of this church is the little word "and" . . . in the weak sense of a mere hyphen, in such expressions as "revelation and reason," "church and culture," "gospel and state," "Bible and science," "theology and philosophy." The anxious purpose always is to give the first element in these expressions a small but guaranteed place alongside the second, or at best to achieve security for it in the protective sphere of the second. . . . Instead of expounding the Bible [it] gives itself with deadly seriousness to the problem of hermeneutics. . . . Instead of speaking the Word entrusted to it, [it] speaks constantly of the speech event. [It] constantly analyzes humanity instead of speaking simply and directly to it. . . . Supposedly to reach people where they are, this church is forever paying regard to them, adjusting itself to them, trying to win their attention and sympathy, attempting to be—or appear to be—as pleasant as possible to them. It is the distracted and therefore the chattering church, the squinting and therefore the stuttering church. . . . It is a church that constantly breaks up afresh into every possible group and party and school and trend. [And if I may second Barth's motion: it is the church of towering babble.]

[pp. 137-39]

And in what is probably his most succinct statement of the case, Barth says:

We believe in the primacy and power of faith, with reference, one hopes, to its pioneer and perfecter (Heb. 12:2), yet every moment we think it appropriate to think and take up positions according to the rules of some self-invented or acquired psychology, politics, aesthetics, or morality unaffected by theological considerations.

Well, did he know the Brethren or didn't he?

CHAPTER NINE

The Party of Parity

After most of this book already was in first draft, the report of a Brethren conference (not at Indianapolis this time) brought me a flash of inspiration. I suddenly realized what is the basic principle that ties together all of today's reductionist, "from below" theology. It is what we shall call "the parity principle"—as its practitioners shall be called "the parity party."

At least among the Brethren, this is not actually "a theology" —in that it is by no means an organized or self-conscious school of thought. Indeed, most "paritists" are theologically disinterested, do not consider themselves theologians, and do not know themselves to have "a theology" other than what they assume to be the common and obvious meaning of the gospel. They do not see theirs as being a system, an innovation, anything that needs to be thought through or defended. They will never have given conscious awareness to what I am proposing is their basic principle. They will never have been concerned as to whether their thought is truly biblical or not. They only believe what is obviously true; the New Testament obviously is true; and thus it goes without saying and without investigation that the New Testament must be in agreement with them. Theirs is, above all, an unexamined theology.

Yet, this also is not "a theology" in another sense. The parity principle, I suggest, is common to a whole host of contemporary theologies that bear separate labels and attract separate constituencies. These would include "liberation theology," "black theology," "feminist theology," "political theology," "process theology," undoubtedly other "named" theologies, plus the host of invisible, nontheological theologies. ("It's unfair to criticize my theology

when I don't even have one!") The Brethren phenomenon this book
has been describing is but the tip of an iceberg.

Although I did not recall the passage until after I had identified the party for myself, Kierkegaard may have been the first to
describe it (in 1855 yet):

> In these times politics is everything. Between this and the
> religious view [by which Kierkegaard means "Christian"] the dif-
> ference is heaven-wide *(toto caelo),* as also the point of departure
> and the ultimate aim differ from it *toto caelo,* since politics
> begins on earth and remains on earth, whereas religion, deriving
> its beginning from above [so that's where Barth got the idea!],
> seeks to explain and transfigure and thereby exalt the earthly to
> heaven. . . . No politics ever has, no politics ever can, no worldli-
> ness ever has, no worldliness ever can, think through or realize to
> its last consequences the thought of human equality. . . . For if
> complete equality were to be attained, worldliness would be at an
> end. But is it not a sort of obsession on the part of worldliness
> that it has got into its head the notion of wanting to enforce com-
> plete equality, and to enforce it by worldly means . . . in a world-
> ly medium? It is only religion that can, with the help of eternity
> [i.e., "from above"], carry human equality to the utmost limit.
> . . . And therefore—be it said to its honor and glory—religion is
> the true humanity [or read: "humanism"].
>
> [*Point of View,* pp. 107-08]

In the interests of euphony, we have chosen the word "parity";
the word "equality"—used by Kierkegaard and the party itself—
comes to the same thing. Equality, Kierkegaard sees, is a crucial
aspect of our becoming truly human—this being the very truth the
party also insists upon. However, because he knows that the true
"equality" which constitutes the one authentic "humanism" is
anything but a worldly ideology centered upon a political principle
of parity, Kierkegaard insists that only Christianity (with its "from
above" orientation) has any chance of getting us there. Consequently, the quarrel is not whether "humanism" (or "equality") is a
good word or a bad one; it is how those words are to be defined and
by whom. Are they "gospel words" or are they "worldly words"?
Kierkegaard contends that the gospel version identifies the one
possibility of our ever becoming either equal or human.

However, the parity party has never caught the distinction and so knows only to push the secular ideology while calling it "Christian"—thus, Kierkegaard would say, cutting itself off from any true realization of the very equalizing and humanizing ideals it espouses. The discussion to follow wants to be understood simply as a biblical exposition of Kierkegaard's idea.

In the ideology of the party, "parity," of course, expresses the ultimate value, the end and goal of human endeavor. Conversely, on the side of "disparity," "dominance" identifies the evil of ultimate threat, and "subordination" the evil of ultimate injustice. Now Christianity obviously does value a form of equality, as Kierkegaard has already suggested and will soon make emphatic. However, consider that the term "dominance" is derived from the Latin *dominus*—meaning "lord," or "master"—and think how essential that concept is to the biblical message. Likewise, regarding "subordination," consider that the *Master's* parting instructions to his disciples included the words: "Whoever would be great among you must be your servant, and whoever would be first among you must be slave of all. For the Son of man came not to be served but to serve." Finally, recall another word from the Upper Room: "You call me Master and Lord; and you are right, for so I am. If I then, your Lord and Master, have washed your feet, you also ought to wash one another's feet."

Clearly, our getting to gospel equality cannot be as simple as eliminating from the faith all titles of lordship or kingship (as a commission of the United Methodist Church has recommended be done). No, ours is the much trickier task of understanding how Jesus can *subordinate* himself to the slave-work of washing feet, while—*in that very act*—claiming the *dominance* of being "Lord." It must be evident that scripture will not easily reduce to a manifesto of simple parity. The gospel's must be a parity that includes and integrates both "dominance" and "subordination"—not one that prohibits them.

Yet, in spite of its abhorrence of "dominance," it is plain that the parity party is very strong on "self-assertiveness." How so? The assumption, I think, is that all or most of us start from a state of having been forced into subordination. (Quite contrary to the

Christian assumption that our problem is that we are sinners, this one locates the problem in our having been sinned against — a most questionable premise). Assertiveness, then, is seen as the proper means for getting oneself up to par. Yet, theoretically, this assertiveness must stop at the level of parity and not drive on into dominance. Whether assertiveness can be that easily controlled is a big question. But again, the very fact that scripture provides so little support for the idea of self-assertiveness indicates that Christian equality is something quite different from what is envisioned by the party.

Yet, Kierkegaard is right that — although it is the farthest thing from an ideological principle — there is a great parity at the heart of the Christian faith:

> But let me give utterance to this which in a sense is my very life, the content of my life for me, its fullness, its happiness, its peace and contentment. There are various philosophies of life which deal with the question of human dignity and human equality. But Christianly, every man (the individual), absolutely every man, once again, absolutely every man is equally near to God. And how is he equally near? Loved by Him. So there is equality, infinite equality between man and man.
>
> [*For Self-Examination*, p. 5]

There are probably few paritists who would be inclined to argue with Kierkegaard's statement — but neither would most of them likely be very impressed by it. They would find it largely irrelevant. Their position would indicate that Kierkegaard has said exactly nothing until that equality before God shows itself in the true, socio-political equalities of this *real* world; and if one has those, who cares whether or not he is also loved *by God?* (Perhaps the basic question behind our whole book is whether "the real world" is the world as it is seen by God "from above" or as seen by man "from below.") But the gospel asks us to seek first the equality of the kingly rule of God and then, if and as they are possible, let socio-political equalities come to us as well. Conversely, the parity party asks us to seek first socio-political equality — often without even taking notice of the equality of being loved by God.

But carrying Kierkegaard a step further, Christianity also would say that all believers have equal standing in Christ, as members of his body—although paritists might get nervous at the implication that there may be unbelievers who do not enjoy such parity. Or again, Christianity would say that, in God's eyes, all are *equally* sinners in need of grace. But the party would come through with a quick "no thank you" on this one; theirs must always be parity *upward* and never downward. Or once more, the cross of Christ is *equally* efficacious for the forgiveness of all. And once more the party would have to say "no thank you"; "forgiveness" has too many overtones of downward parity. The party, in this case, would prefer to speak of God's equal "acceptance" of all—which move, of course, also eliminates the need for repentance or any sort of atonement, whether through the cross or in any other way.

So the fact is that, although the gospel does include very basic instances of parity, it will never make parity a dogmatic principle in the way the party does. There are too many points at which the gospel has to speak of downward parity and even introduce some vitally important "disparities." Consequently, the parity principle is seen to be an alien idea, a derivative of secular humanism rather than the true humanism of the gospel.

As we proceed to spot the many different ways in which the parity principle influences contemporary Christian thought, it surely is the case that not every paritist accepts every application. Yet, my guess is that there is a broad consistency and agreement. What follows would stand as a quite accurate statement of faith for a great many people.

Undoubtedly, the most fundamental thrust toward parity—though hardly the most visible one—is the effort to equalize the relationship between God and man. We have seen different evidences of this in earlier chapters. Such leveling can and does proceed by two different means: man can assert himself up toward parity with God, or he can bring God down to parity with himself. First, human self-exaltation.

The scripture most used here is the Genesis verse about our being created in "the image of God." That one is welcomed, because it implies a certain parity between ourselves and God, as well as with one another. The only difficulty is—actually, the only *three* difficulties are: (1) Now we dare never read the Bible beyond its first chapter; because scripture goes on to specify that that image proved not to be an indelible endowment, that the status of our creation is not something we automatically can claim as present truth about ourselves. Indeed, Paul says that in Adam all *die,* that our God-image has died—and his verse is just as biblical as the one from Genesis. (2) Although it is regularly understood otherwise, the Genesis verse does not say that each human individual is created in the image of God. It says that "man," the human *corporation,* was—and that is a different idea. And (3) it is unlikely that the term "image" ever was meant to carry the parity overtones the party gives to it. In a following chapter, the serpent's phrase, "You shall be *like God,"* is a much more promising candidate for parity interpretation. And, of course, it isn't very smart to premise Christian theology on the words of a snake.

Perhaps the biblical reference that truly comes closest to suggesting a parity between God and man is Psalm 8:5, in which we are told that man was made "little less than God, crowned with glory and honor." Of course, there is still the problem of whether the fact of creation can be taken as a guarantee of present status; but the Psalm itself poses an even greater problem. The refrain with which it both opens and closes reads: "O Lord, our Lord, how majestic is *thy name* in all the earth!" In verse 4, there is the question, "What is man that thou art mindful of him?"—an expression of some skepticism, if not outright disparagement. And even verse 5 reads, "Yet *thou has made him* little less than God." The Psalmist is intent solely on exalting *God* for what he has done, not on exalting *man* for what he is. The Psalmist's true interest is in establishing a great *disparity.* God is the Creator; and man—however great he may be—is a creature, the credit for whom belongs entirely to the Creator and not to man himself. And thus the Psalmist takes his stand, not with the paritists, but right alongside the biblical disparitists who talk about pots not answering back to the potter (Romans 9:21, Jeremiah 18:4, Isaiah 64:8) and axes not setting themselves up against the hewer (Isaiah 10:15). The Bible has no interest in the cause of human self-assertiveness.

However, at those times when the party takes thought and acts with theological deliberation, the movement is more likely the reverse one of bringing God down to the human level. This is the

"Christianity as a religion" approach described in our first chapter. Now the assumption is made that, whatever we are told of God in scripture (and accordingly, whatever we ourselves might identify as God and accept him as being) is actually a product of the creative religious experience of a particular human culture—a *mythologoumenon,* as Karl Barth so impressively put it.

It follows that, if the people of Bible times got to decide what God should be for them, we have an equal right to say what he should be for us now. That's parity. It is true, of course, that some parity theologians are willing to say this more forthrightly than are others; but most seem to imply it even while hedging on the matter. Still, this ploy does make for fine parity: we can continue to grant a certain verbal dominance to God (singing the old hymns, reading scripture, etc.) even while being secure in the knowledge that we are the ones who defined him so in the first place. God is now as dependent upon our defining (if not creating) him as we are dependent upon his creating us—a true interdependence.

Yet, no matter what rationale they may give to their action, it appears that paritists, without question, simply see equality with God as a thing to be grasped—whether Jesus saw it so or not. The equality grab shows up in ways such as these: God can be defined in impersonal terms of process, force, spirit, energy, creativity, presence, or whatever—rather than by the personal metaphors regularly used in the Bible. One person prefers a parity term, "the community of God," in place of the disparate "kingdom of God" and so proceeds to reword the scripture. Another decides that, although scripture consistently portrays God as masculine, we find the truth to be better served by making him "beyond gender." Still another proposes that, although both Jesus and different New Testament writers teach us to address God as "Father," we, in our wisdom, can feel free to ignore that counsel. Once, when leading the Church of the Brethren Annual Conference in prayer, the moderator inadvertently fell into the biblical style of addressing God as "Father." He consequently caught so much static that he felt compelled to come back at another session to explain himself.

Plainly, all cases of this sort assume that it is our prerogative to define God to our liking, in accord with our religious experience—this, rather than God's defining himself for us through scripture. But that's parity.

So when it comes to this very crucial matter of knowing
God — who he is and who he wants to be for us — there are two completely opposite approaches. The "religious" view (from below)
starts from the assumption that God *is* (if we grant that much) and
can be found within the sphere of human reality — just as, for instance, gold is present in the crust of the earth. It is the case, then,
that, in their religious questing, the ancient Hebrews *discovered*
God — just as someone, once upon a time, discovered gold. Consequently, out of their store of cultural images, these Hebrews then
chose the figures, analogies, metaphors, titles, and attributions that
would best relate him to their particular experiences and needs —
making him that God which will be "most meaningful to us," as
they would have said had they spoken parity lingo. The ancient
Hebrews did this for God just as surely as human beings also did it
for gold — deciding that gold should be called "gold," that it should
be deemed "beautiful," "precious," appropriate for wedding rings
or whatever. The gold, of course, just sat there; all of these meaningful attributions are entirely our own doing. And so it is that
religion approaches God. Yet, we need to be aware that this way
comes perilously close to signifying that "we are the potters; you,
God, are the clay."

The Bible, just as clearly, has things precisely the other way
around. God (now entirely *active)* shows personal initiative and
dominance in coming to and confronting us. In that situation, we
certainly do not volunteer to define him. The most we can or
should do is ask, "Who are you?" In fact, this question itself is out
of order. Even if he offered to answer, there is no possibility we
could *comprehend* him, get a mental hold on him, or throw a mental line around him (which is what the word "comprehend" means).
No, the Bible asserts that no one has "seen" God. It commands that
we shall not even attempt to make an image of him. And when
Moses tried the question of "Who are you?" God rebuffed him with
an "I am who I am" ("That's my business, not yours"). This
religious audacity of our defining a god to suit our own needs and
experience is the last thing the Bible will countenance.

So we don't even ask the impertinent question, "Who are
you?" We ask, "How would you have us think of you? Speak,
Lord, for thy servant heareth." And the answers in scripture are
presented as being God's own answers, not as creations of Hebrew

culture. Of course, the answers come in the form of human, culture-created words—how else could God ever communicate to human, culture-created people? But that doesn't prohibit it from being God who decided which words would best communicate what he wanted to communicate. If scripture is considered to be inspired, to be a rule of faith at any point, certainly it must be here where God speaks about himself.

None of God's words are to be taken as answering the ontological question, "Who are you?" So scripture does not tell us that God actually is a male—anymore than it tells us that he is actually a king, a shepherd, a rock, a fortress, or anything else. But it doesn't tell us that he is beyond gender, or some impersonal force of nature, either. We cannot know—and have no need to know—who God is in and for himself. However, he does tell us a good deal about his own function and character—and particularly the nature of his relationship to ourselves. He does, for example, say, in effect, "You will be closer the mark to think of me as a king rather than as creative process, to think of me as masculine rather than as a neuterized something-or-other beyond gender."

But more, God will not even allow us to make his identity a problem we can consider without considering our own identity at the same time. Every one of the biblical answers (or at least those that are reiterated and given emphasis) say as much about who *we* are as they do about who God is. God will not define himself except in relation to us, will not define himself without defining us as well. In effect, "You cannot know who I am except by also coming to know who you are." Thus, quite to the contrary of the religious approach, not only are we prohibited from defining God, we don't even get to define ourselves.

But catch the pattern. Perhaps most striking, though obviously not the most frequent: "If I am the Potter, you are the clay." But then, also: "If I am Judge, you are the judged, i.e., one who needs to be and assuredly will be justified." "If I am Lord, you are liege." "If I am King, you are subject." "If I am Father, you are child." "If I am Shepherd, you are sheep." "If I am Wooer, you are the wooed." "If I am Husband, you are wife."

What all of this says is that the Bible does in no way support the parity principle of human religion and its culturally derived "God-concepts." All of the modern attempts to go this way must be seen as direct violations of our rule of faith and practice. Rather, we should thank God for that essential *disparity* which is his "holiness" — an earlier chapter having taught us that that is precisely what the word means.

We need, at this point, perhaps, an excursus on how to read the Bible. By this time it is obvious that I do not buy the view that the Bible is wholly human cultural creation with nothing of divine revelation about it. Perhaps I have been read, however, as suggesting the opposite, that the Bible is wholly divine revelation with nothing of cultural creation about it. Well, I don't believe that, either. Neither traditional Brethrenism nor this book have argued for such a fundamentalist view of scripture. No, the Bible (I believe) is a mix of revelatory and cultural elements.

But on what grounds, then, does one draw the distinction between the eternal truth of God's self-revelation and the relative and transient concepts of cultural bias? It will not do (as the paritists presently are doing) to take the ideas we like as being revelatory and authoritative and reject the ones we don't like as being cultural inventions we are free to ignore or change. That approach makes *us,* our cultural bias, the rule of the Bible rather than its being our rule. It will not do, either, to set up the parity principle as the test. Again, that principle is the invention of *our* particular culture, a reflection of *our* bias, not a rule set up by, or derived from, scripture itself.

What I propose, then, is that those ideas which recur frequently, whose importance scripture itself points up through consistency, reiteration, emphasis, enlargement, and placement — that these be granted the importance the Bible itself attributes to them and thus be accepted as authoritative revelation. On the other hand, what the Bible itself shows to be unimportant — by treating in a spasmodic, inconsistent, desultory way — this we are free (and even obligated) to accept in the same spirit, as being of only incidental, cultural interest. It is as unbiblical to emphasize what scripture treats as unimportant as it is to play down and disregard what scripture treats as important. But letting scripture orchestrate its own message is, I suggest, the one way truly to use the Bible as a *rule* of faith and practice.

Thus, because the thesis of Ecclesiastes that "all is vanity" is confined to that one book of the Bible and is so contradictory to what is taught and assumed everywhere else, we (although needing to remember that the book is there and deserves a hearing) safely can take it as the reflection of a particular cultural influence rather than a fundamental proposition of "the message of the Bible."

Likewise, the cult of animal sacrifice is big — in a restricted sector of the Old Testament. However, the Old Testament prophets themselves begin to disparage cultic sacrifice (as we, in Chapter Two, found Amos and Micah doing). It does not manage to make the leap into the New Testament. The early church rejects it, and Judaism itself soon drops it. Undeniably, animal sacrifice is in the Bible; yet the Bible itself as much as tells us that it was something relative to a particular culture and not an aspect of the eternal truth of God. On its own, scripture leads us to make the distinction and even guides us in the making of it.

However, the case is quite otherwise when, for example, we consider the instruction that we are to know and address God as "Father." That idea builds, rather than dwindles, through the course of the Old Testament. It flowers rather than fails with Jesus and the New Testament. The usage is frequent and consistent in virtually (perhaps absolutely) every book of the New Testament. And most important, it is "placed" as being entirely crucial: It is Jesus' first word in response to the disciples' question, "How should we pray?" The early church gave the usage such importance that it made the effort to retain Jesus' own Aramaic term *Abba* even after the church's language had shifted to Greek — thus enabling Paul, in what is plainly intended as a statement of great significance, to write, "But when the time had fully come, God sent forth his Son, born of a woman, born under the law, so that we might receive adoption as sons. And because you are sons, God has sent the Spirit of his Son into our hearts, crying, '*Abba!* Father!' So through God you are no longer a slave but a son, and if a son then an heir" [Galatians 4:4-7].

Consequently, when, under the parity principle (gender parity this time), the party spots "Father" as a cultural aberration that has to go, the case is entirely different from what it was with Ecclesiastes or with animal sacrifice. And whoever works such changes simply cannot claim to be using the New Testament as a rule of faith and practice.

We had to spend that much space on the party's attempt to level God and man, because the issue is so fundamental. But of course, parity must be applied to Jesus as well as to God. Jesus, now, must not be treated as though he were any more than one of us. This attitude has been evident among the Brethren for some time—not particularly as a theological proposition but simply through a disinclination to present him in the terms the New Testament does or to credit him as anything more than our Great Teacher, the Model Human. At times the leveling has been done by playing with words, "Yes, Jesus is Son of God, but so are we all"—which obviously is not the New Testament intention of the phrase "Son of God." Or again, "Yes, it is proper to identify Jesus as 'Christ,' if you are ready to grant similar status to Gandhi, Martin Luther King, and others"—although one must disregard a great deal of New Testament teaching to manage this.

But in our day, not only is Christ's deity downplayed but also his incomparable humanity. Jesus was a social revolutionary pure and simple, who never said or did anything to suggest that there might be any supernatural dimension either to himself or to history—I once heard a prominent feminist theologian argue. Jesus as much needed to have his racial prejudice corrected by the Canaanite woman as she to have her daughter healed by him—I heard reported from another. (Such an interpretation of Matthew 15:21-28 does establish parity between Jesus and the woman. But what makes it completely incredible is that, if such were the meaning, the early church would have preserved the incident and Matthew included it in his Gospel—a Gospel dedicated to portraying an entirely disparitous Jesus. No, the passage makes much better sense, not as the woman's correcting Jesus' prejudice, but as Jesus' correcting that of the disciples by letting them hear the enormity of it when, from his own lips, comes the prejudice they as much asked him to express.) As plain as can be, any parity-interpretation of Jesus necessarily involves a renunciation of the New Testament rule of faith.

Coming now to human-level relationships, one of the frequently heard claims of the party is that of parity among the world religions: "Yes, Christianity is the true faith *for us,* but Islam (or any other religion) is just as much the true faith for its followers." This, again, is an attractive idea. However, the evidence is overwhelming that the New Testament at large teaches as being integral to God's self-revelation what John 14:6 states explicitly, "No one comes to the Father, but by me." (By the way, it does not follow from this that other religions are to be scorned, ridiculed, or dismissed as devoid of truth.) So, again, parity can be taught only by playing false any commitment to our professed rule of faith and practice.

In the party's attitude toward world religions, we get a clue to the major shift of focus that comes with the parity principle. Normally (and biblically) "truth" denotes objective realities existing and having their validity quite apart from the proclivities or perceptions of the observer. So, for example, the Bible means to affirm that God's actions can best be described as those of a "Father" whether or not anyone ever accepts the idea, likes it, finds it meaningful, or whatever. Our opinion of it has nothing to do with whether a claim is true or not.

Yet, with the parity party inevitably comes the subjectivistic redefinition, "true *for me.*" The switch makes paritistic sense. As long as truth is understood objectively, there obviously is going to be a great disparity among possessors of the truth. One religion will be truer, have more of the truth, than others do. Some people surely know more things (and more important things) than other people do. Some people have a better knowledge of the Bible, of theology, of Christianity, than others do. Yet, with the party, such disparity simply cannot be endured—the implication that one person possesses more of the truth than another. However, if it were that *the* truth is that which is true *for me,* the disparity would immediately disappear: "I am as much 'of the truth' as anyone, for who are you to say what is or what is not true *for me?*"

The truth now shifts from being objective, public, and testable to being subjectivistic, relative, and unquestionable. Thus, truth also loses its communicability and its communal character in the process of becoming individualistic, atomistic, and isolated: that something is true *for you* says nothing at all as to whether it is also true for me. And with this, there also comes a shift from valuing the *product* to valuing the *process*.

For example, traditionally the value of poetry has been found in the product — the objective, "discussable" quality of the poem a poet produced. The problem with this approach is that it immediately exposes great disparities. There is William Shakespeare. Then there are a number of other poets in spitting distance of him. Then there are great numbers who aren't within a stone's throw. And finally there is the host which no one can count who are such poor poets that they can't even understand why Shakespeare should be rated as better than they are. ("You should never call anyone a 'poor poet.' It's the same as calling him a poor *person*. Remember that his poems are very meaningful to him.")

Of course, the easy way out of poetic disparagement is to move the evaluation from the product to the process. Now poetry is valued for the poetic feeling, the aesthetic experience, that comes to one in the process of poeticizing. Parity is ours: "You may criticize my poem; yet you can't say but that I have felt just as poetic as Shakespeare ever did. I know what it is to be a *poet* — and you will never deny me that!"

You're right; I won't, and I wouldn't even want to. In fact, I like to think that Shakespeare produced his sublime measures without feeling anything at all — except tired when he was done. I know that is how my writing leaves me — and it would give me satisfaction to know he paid the same price for his (that's parity). My guess is that the Old Testament *prophets* were so busy in thinking through their message and getting it out that they couldn't even tell you what it "feels" like to be inspired of God. Inspiration is important for what it produces, not what it feels like.

Now I am not particularly bothered by the idea of parity poetry, as long as I don't have to read the products of these aesthetic orgies. But when it comes to parity theology, I am. Yet, the Brethren have imported "subjective process" even into the study of scripture.

I attended a denominationally-sponsored Bible seminar. We did not engage any significant issues — did not address the matter of the Bible's being our rule of faith and practice, did not ask what it means to call it "the word of God" or how we might best hear it as such, did not talk about "rightly dividing the word of truth" or what truth is to be found when one does rightly divide it. No, we learned techniques for arousing wide participation and helping people have "a good experience" in Bible study. All process; very little product.

It turned out that the key to people's having a good experience is to give them all 'A's—that is, maintain absolute parity and never suggest the possibility that anyone's understanding of scripture might be truer than someone else's. The last thing to do is use scripture as a "rule" and start measuring people's faith or practice.

Three particular techniques were demonstrated and tried. The first was meditation. From John, Jesus' words about his being the vine and we the branches were read. We then were led into a meditative frame of mind and asked to form mental images of meadows, vines, branches, grapes, etc.—even, then, drawing on paper a picture of what we had seen. And this was it. Of course, it can be taken as axiomatic that each person's experience was true and beautiful *for him.*

Now I have had enough training in biofeedback and relaxation techniques to know about brainwave frequencies, the different sides of the brain, et al.—and to know the psycho-physical validity of mental relaxation and self-hypnosis. However, I also know that, from beginning to end, the Holy Scriptures consist of "words"—words intended to communicate specific cognitive meanings, words that must be understood either correctly or incorrectly according to that intention. I also know that nowhere in scripture does "meditation" mean phasing out one's rational mind in order to enjoy subjective psychological process. There, "meditation" is the seeking of cognitive product—using one's mind to ponder the word, to hear a definite, content-filled message from God. And even though this method inevitably will create disparities of truth, I don't think anything else rates as Bible study.

The second technique was closest to right. Each person worked at finding an outline in the book of Micah. Very good; that involved a cognitive effort to discover objective truth. The only difficulty was that it stopped short: "Everybody gets an 'A'; your outline has as much chance of being right as anyone else's."

I have no problem with this technique as a good preliminary to Bible study—if it then be followed by a group effort (involving some consultation of scholarly opinion) aimed at achieving the truest possible outline and interpretation of Micah. But the opinion was rendered that the point of the exercise was to have each person feel as though he can do Bible study with the experts — no disparity allowed (and no "rule of faith" either).

The third technique was a case study in which the idea was to find a situation in scripture that is ambiguous as possible, an ethical dilemma in which there is no clear guidance — so that the participants will have to argue the matter out for themselves. Here, we deliberately avoided any possibility of a rule of faith and practice, because we wanted scripture only to set the question. We, on our own, were to find the answer. So, in this case, we debated whether or not ancient Israel should have instituted a monarchy.

I personally had my doubts whether the scripture is as ambiguous as we made it out to be. If you start with God and Samuel's reluctance in the matter, go to Saul's failure and the sad story of David (recounted in one of our earlier chapters), and then follow the even sadder succession through to its bitter end in the Babylonian exile; if you pick up the prophetic promise of a coming kingly Messiah and follow it through to the one known as the King of the Jews who specified that his kingdom was not of this world — well then, it seems to me that scripture has a rather clear word about what can be hoped for from kingdoms of this world in contrast to kingdoms not of this world.

But all this was disallowed. Scripture was not to give answers, because we wanted to have a discussion in which our opinions were seen to be as valid as any. And because, plainly, the question as to whether ancient Israel should have had a monarchy is at least somewhat irrelevant, we were to transpose our discussion to a related topic of more interest, say, authority in the home. So we had a good experience and everybody got 'A's; but I still fail to see how scripture was fairly presented as scripture or how anyone was helped to know the Bible as the word of God or a rule of anything.

Yet, I am convinced that it is here, in this obsession for the parity of experiential process, lies the source of much current Brethren antiintellectualism, our biblical and theological disinterest. We hate the idea of disparity: "And why should I give attention to Markus Barth? I have the same Bible he has and can read it as well as he can. So he reads his and finds that Paul was strong on exhomologesis. Big deal! I read mine and find that Paul really loused up the simple gospel of Jesus. And I have just as much right to my reading as Barth does to his. That's parity."

"And why, above all, should I give attention to Papa Barth, a *theologian?* After all, theology is a matter of one's personal religious experience. And I dare anyone to say I am not every bit as close to God and have known as much of him as has Karl Barth or anyone else. When Barth talks about 'the church in defect' he is only expressing his own opinion—and I have just as much right to mine, namely, that Barth is all wet. Besides, how can you *criticize* a person's *theology?* His personal ideas are very precious to him. And if those are the ideas that speak to him, how can you say they are untrue? That's not parity."

"How can you criticize a person's theology?" I don't know. All I know is that I have been laying mine out before the Brethren (and non-Brethren) for thirty years now, and people haven't found any difficulty in getting it criticized. I think the meaning must be that you can't criticize the theology of a paritist whose truth is not intended to be objective and public but is simply the affirmation of what is true for him. That's parity. In any case, among us you can criticize the preacher's dress or his delivery—but not his theology (those ideas are precious to him).

For the parity party, the end and goal of Christianity is "religious experience." And in our day, the most influential voice in this regard is probably that of the noted psychologist, Abraham Maslow. Maslow begins by denying that there is any "above" from which anything possibly could come. It follows, then, that religion must consist in, can consist of nothing other than, psychological experience—altered states of consciousness which he calls "peak experiences." And these are always and everywhere phenomenologically [18 letters, in English, by Eller] the same—quite apart from whatever self-invented belief-structure the religionist may attach to them. Identical, also, are the peak experiences of those who are presumably nonreligious—whether those experiences are induced by drugs, by sexual stimulation, or in any number of other ways.

Maslow does qualify that only those peak experiences are valid that have good consequences for the individual's personal development and his life in society. But this isn't much help, because he doesn't say where we are to get the standards for deciding what are "good" consequences (not "from above," obviously) or who is to do the deciding. He has no way out of his subjectivism: If Adolf Hitler (with the support of the German people) says his peak experiences — of which his political rallies would be an example — had good consequences for himself and his society, who is Maslow to say otherwise?

Maslow then proceeds (1) to preempt the terminology religion customarily has used in reference to that which is "from above" (e.g., "spiritual," "faith," "the transcendent," "the holy," and even such words as "sin," "prayer," "salvation," et al.); (2) to reduce these to purely psychological reference; (3) to assert that such is what those words have always meant, is the only meaning they could carry; and then (4) to claim that he has scientifically proven religion to be nothing more than a particular type of universal psychological experience.

Now the very attractive thing Maslow has achieved is total religious parity. Anyone — be he atheist, pagan, secularist, Satanist, hedonist — anyone is (or can be) just as truly religious as anyone else. Neither Moses, Isaiah, nor Jesus have anything on you. They had their peak experiences; you have had yours; and nothing else has any reality.

Now whether or not the entire parity party goes all the way with Maslow, it does buy his basic assumption. If your faith produces good religious experience, it is a true faith — whatever else could be the test? Whatever I experience as good *is* good. And whatever makes me feel bad obviously must *be* bad. There is no need for anyone to face me with objective evidence or rational arguments demonstrating otherwise. Good is good and bad is bad — this I *know,* because my feelings tell me so.

So, for the paritists, the real test of any faith is the religious experience accompanying it. My religious experience is the ultimate truth *for me.* This is truth apprehended and evaluated by my infallible "feelings." Parity, then, lies in the fact that every other person's feelings are equally infallible for him. And if, otherwise, truth be taken as that which is apprehended and evaluated by the reasoning mind, all sorts of disparity arise, and some people might even turn out to be *wrong*.

Yet, in this instance as earlier, the parity principle is found to work precisely contrary to our rule of faith and practice. "Peak experiences" are the end and goal of religious faith. That, of course, is Abraham Maslow speaking and not Abraham the Father of Faith. However, let's test the hypothesis by going with Abraham to his peak experience on Mt. Moriah. What the Bible will there make clear is that peak experiences are not valued for themselves; they are only "means" (the process), valued solely for the "fruit" (the product) they bear.

"Tell us about Mt. Moriah, Abraham."

"Well, Dr. Maslow, God came from above and met me there. And there I learned from him that it is good for us to obey him even when, for ourselves, we can't figure out why he has asked what he has. There I learned that 'the Lord will provide'—which is why I gave the peak that name. And there I learned that our God does not want human sacrifices the way other gods do. And I can tell you that my learning those things through the crisis of almost sacrificing my son was an experience I will never forget."

"Would you say it was a 'peak experience'?"

"Sure, on Mt. Moriah, what else?"

"Great, let me write down that Abraham had a peak experience."

"But why don't you also write down all that other stuff I told you?"

"No, I can't use that. That isn't scientific evidence. You yourself said it was all 'from above.' It's only the fact you had a peak experience we're after."

But in the Bible, it is Moses and not Abraham who is the real authority on peak experiences. Sinai #1, with its burning bush, undoubtedly was a great one for Moses. Yet, what he may or may not have "felt" on that occasion is entirely beside the point. The experience was significant only because it eventuated in getting the children of Israel out of slavery. Sinai #2, with its tablets, must also have been great. But we'll never know, because the only interest is in getting Israel into the covenant and under the law. Pisgah marks the only peak experience designed for Moses' own benefit—and whether or not that had good consequences, who can say? The experience itself killed him; about one peak experience of that sort would be enough for anybody.

The purpose behind the Mount of Transfiguration "peak" was to reveal to the disciples who Jesus really was (and when Peter wanted to "affirm his own experience" by witnessing to the fact that it made him feel good about himself, Jesus was quick to set him straight). Pentecost: to set the church upon its evangelistic mission. Paul on the Damascus Road: to make him the Apostle of Jesus Christ to the Gentiles. And it is probably Paul who best states the truth of the matter: "If your glossolalic peak experience doesn't get you obedient to God in the building up of the church, forget it."

Our rule of faith and practice never values peak experiences for themselves. How they make you "feel" is beneath notice. No, by their "fruits" you shall know them. And fruits are objective, public results whose truth can be tested and evaluated; they are not inner infallibilities.

Consider people such as Moses, Elijah, Jeremiah, and Jesus. It is by no means plain that these were "persons who felt good about themselves." Jeremiah testified that being God's prophet gave him a pain in the gut (Jeremiah 20:9); Moses said he would rather die (Numbers 11:15); Elijah actually tried to cop out (1 Kings 19:3); and even Jesus had a strong preference that the cup pass him by (Luke 22:42).

At one point, Jeremiah accuses God of having raped him (that is the real meaning of the word used in Jeremiah 20:7). We can know for a fact that the prophet "felt" ravaged. ("But did you actually do that to him, Lord?" "Of course not! And he doesn't really believe it, either. But don't you say anything against my boy Jeremiah. He's *doing* all right. And it isn't easy to be a human, at the mercy of a bunch of crazy, mixed up feelings. It could be he will feel just the opposite in another chapter or so." [Actually, it is just six *verses* later that Jeremiah says: "Sing to the Lord; praise the Lord! For he has delivered the life of the needy from the hand of evildoers."])

God apparently doesn't care a great deal about how his saints are *feeling*—as long as they are *doing*. He regularly acts only to keep them going, not to make them feel better. Feeling good about yourself is no proof that you are right with God, or that he feels good about you. Feeling unhappy is no proof of anything, either. It is as wrong to take *peak* experiences as denoting the very truth of things as it is to take *depth* experiences that way. Maslow himself recognizes that it is impossible to distinguish drug and otherwise induced peaks from religious ones. No, it is only by their "fruits" you can know them.

So the only question is whether you are *doing* the will of God, regardless of your feelings of the moment. It would seem that God knows our feelings are not "of the truth"; but are rather the most fallible faculties we possess. Perhaps, then, he would have us be more in touch with *him* than with our own feelings, our bodies, our selves—he being the somewhat more reliable guide to truth. In fact, he would probably be happy to have us forget about our feelings and think only of him. And who knows, we just might find ourselves feeling better in the very process.

It could be that the faith isn't even particularly interested in the parity—the narcissistic parity—of the right of every person to feel good (and religious) about himself. It could be that faith's only real interest is that *God's* will be done on earth as it is in heaven. And it could be that our precious "feelings" have very little to do with *that* truth of things, one way or another. It could be that the "theology of feelings" is clear off the biblical track.

Perhaps the point at which the party's parity principle becomes most visible (although not, by that token, any more influential than elsewhere) is in its "social ethics," i.e., its concept of *justice*. Kierkegaard observed that it is in politics that "equality" becomes such a prominent term. And it is self-evident that the party—with its black, feminist, liberation theologies and all—is very big on social justice. That is totally commendable, and I have absolutely no criticism to make in this regard.

However, my argument will be that the party's concept of justice is derived, not from scripture (as per our Chapters Six and Seven), but from modern, democratic, secular political theory. As Kierkegaard said, "In these times politics is everything." Yet neither I nor (I am confident) Kierkegaard mean to say that, because it comes from a secular source, the ideal of social equality must be a bad one. Indeed, I am ready to say (and hope I can be heard as saying) that it is the best and highest ideal to which secular aspiration can attain. May God bless the world in its striving for human equality. Nevertheless, this is not what the biblical revelation intends as "justice."

In *The Cost of Discipleship,* again, Bonhoeffer picks up on two words of Jesus from the Sermon on the Mount: "For I say unto you, that except your righteousness shall *exceed* that of the scribes and Pharisees, ye shall in no wise enter the kingdom of heaven" (pp. 135 & 140-41) and "If ye salute your brethren only, what do ye *more than* others" (pp. 162 & 169-71). The Greek word, in both instances, is *perissos*—that which exceeds, the "more than," the extraordinary, the peculiar. And the point, clearly, is not that Jesus is objecting to the righteousness of the scribes and Pharisees or the saluting of one's brethren—but that Christian discipleship dare never settle for even the best behavior of the world but must always press on to its peculiar norm and standard. And our search, now, is for the "extraordinary justice" of the gospel.

It will take me some pages and even a move into our next section before I can get the distinction fully delineated, so I beg your patience and careful attention.

Regarding the world's "parity justice," the "equal rights" out of "Equal Rights Amendment" says it best: "equal rights (that's parity)" is a synonym for "justice." And such is the language of our political tradition, beginning perhaps with the American Revolution, then the French, and following straight on through: "all men are created equal," "with liberty and justice *for all,*" "Liberty, Equality, Fraternity," "equal under the law," "equal opportunity employer," "equal pay for equal work." "Justice" begins and ends in parity.

There is no denying that this is a noble ideal. However, our rule of extraordinary faith and practice is also big on justice—as some of our earlier chapters have made evident. But as we saw there, its understanding of justice is quite different from that of our secular western legal and political tradition. And there was no evidence that it is constructed upon the principle of parity. Rather than "the achievement of parity," the biblical concept of justice is "God's getting things made right, according to what he calls right and considers the right means for getting them that way." And God's "right" dare not automatically be taken as a synonym for the human concept of "parity."

To this point, we have identified the principle of secular-political "justice" as being "parity" and have argued that the biblical principle is different from that. However, our treatment is incomplete in that we have not said what this different biblical principle actually is. "God's definition of right"—but what may that be? We can best address this question by introducing another point of contrast between parity theology and biblical theology—this having to do with their respective concepts of "community."

We should recognize, first, that "justice" and "community" are not entirely separate matters. Neither can exist in the absence of the other. Any lack of justice will prevent community from being complete and true. Any effort toward justice that does not eventuate in community has not yet reached its goal. The two may not quite be synonymous, but they have to be simultaneous.

Now the parity party and the biblical rule are together in at least *speaking* strongly of "community." Yet, I will argue that this is the point at which they most strongly speak *past* each other. We have arrived at what may be the most basic divergence between the two points of view.

If the parity party does not actually equate "community" and "parity," it does clearly make parity the ground of community: Community is based upon parity. Community follows from parity. There is no reason even to talk about community until parity is established among its potential members. And disparity, on the other hand, is anticommunity, the death of community.

Yet, the Bible does not recognize this principle at all. Rather than being based upon "parity," its community is based upon what we shall call "voluntary subordination"—a term anathema to any idea of parity. The two views are at loggerheads.

As the rubric of the biblical position, in relation to which all else falls into place, I propose the words of Jesus in Mark 8:34-35:

> If any man would come after me, let him deny himself and take up his cross and follow me. For whoever would save his life will lose it; and whoever loses his life for my sake and the gospel will save it.

Everything about this passage indicates that it is intended (by

Jesus, by the early church, and by the Gospel writer) as an essential statement of principle. The theme is self-denial and the voluntary losing of one's life. "The cross" is introduced as the paradigm of the idea — even though the significance of the reference cannot become apparent until after Jesus' own death. And indeed, the paradox that the losing of one's life can be the saving of it as much as requires his resurrection. All of which is to say what the further development of the principle will make clear, namely, that voluntary subordination is not a self-contained, self-evident, self-operative bit of wisdom — as is the parity principle. It assumes and requires the death and resurrection of Jesus as its basis — even if the Gospel has to get ahead of itself in saying so. The requirement of voluntary subordination has to come "from above" rather than from the below of democratic political theory.

As the one statement of the idea best emphasizing its contrast with "parity," I propose the hymn Paul uses in Philippians 2:5-11:

> Have this mind among yourselves, which you have in Christ Jesus, who, though he was in the form of God, did not count equality . . . a thing to be grasped, but emptied himself, taking the form of a servant. . . . He humbled himself and became obedient unto death, even death on a cross. Therefore, God has highly exalted him.

Paul here takes what earlier had probably been a hymn in praise of Christ and transforms it into an ethical injunction: "Have this mind among yourselves." Self-subordinating servanthood can happen only when we are in Christ and because we have taken his mind for our own. And even then, it is specifically a participation in his death and resurrection, never anything other than that.

Yes, I know the text itself reads that he "did not count equality *with God* a thing to be grasped." But I also know that, in emptying himself, Jesus became not only a servant *to God* but to every human being as well. So, particularly if this is also to be the mind *in us,* there is no other way to read the text than as a renunciation of parity as ever being a thing to be grasped on any level. Christ Jesus, the hymn says, began by being completely disparate from us ("in the form of God"), emptied himself into the disparity of the humiliated servant's death on a cross, and then was exalted into the ultimate disparity of "the name which is above very name." There simply is no room in that pattern for anything like parity—yet, we are told specifically that *this* is the mind we should have among ourselves.

As the statement most detailed and helpful in getting the subordination principle applied to us, I propose Galatians 2:20:

> I have been crucified with Christ; it is no longer I who live, but Christ who lives in me; and the life I now live in the flesh I live by faith in the Son of God, who loved me and gave himself for me.

This passage is one with the foregoing: our self-denial, our self-subordination, must be understood as a participation in the death and resurrection of Christ. In this verse, "the life I now live" (following my being crucified with Christ) can be nothing other than what Paul elsewhere is quick to identify as the life of being resurrected with Christ. Yet, here, Paul's use of the word "I" suggests a new line of thought.

We earlier called the parity principle the highest concept of "justice" of which secular society is capable. Here we can say that the parity principle is also the highest concept of "community" available to the world. And why is this so? Because a basic fact of human existence is that all our problems of injustice, lack of community, and gross disparity of all sorts can be attributed to the thrust of human *ego* (the "I"). This is the engine that drives human history and has brought us to where we are—this compulsion that resists any sort of subordination and ever pushes toward dominance. It is human ego that creates and maintains all the disparities that plague our life together.

The ideal of parity, then, signifies nothing other than a human effort to *control* ego. Ego is there and is going to be there; so the best we can hope for is that it be put under constraint by creating a ceiling. Ego, now, is recognized, affirmed, and even demanded as the self-assertiveness that is to oppose all subordination of one's self, all dominance on the part of others. *But* (and here is the crucial point) that ego drive is to push only to the level of parity— that far and no farther. This, then, is the state of equilibrium—of "equal rights," "equal opportunity," "equal distribution," etc., that the world calls "justice." It is hard to imagine what other goal for society could even be envisioned. Certainly controlled ego is infinitely better than uncontrolled ego would be. And when all we have to work with is human ego, what alternative is there?

Granted, this parity principle has its problems. It remains to be seen how close humanity can ever come to achieving true parity. We have made some gains (at least on some points), although our overall record is not what could be called "good"; and our gains on one front are very often counterbalanced by our losses on others. For one thing, it is a very chancy business to encourage the upward assertion of ego and then decree that it stop at a given point—even if we had a reliable way of locating that point. I am not saying we have any other option; but there is here a very real difficulty.

Another difficulty lies in defining "parity." One man's parity is another woman's subordination. Who is to say what is "parity"? Is being "the same" the only way of being "equal"? Is becoming "just like men" the only way for women to gain parity with them? And on what grounds was it determined that being a homemaker is not equal to holding a paying job? I am not being sarcastic; these are very complicated questions. And, of course, questions of this sort arise regarding not only gender parity but any sort of parity you might suggest. The parity principle may be the best we can do; but it is no magic answer to anything.

However, if the parity principle is a difficult answer, the biblical principle is no answer at all. Galatians 2:20 echoes what the other texts have been saying; and I understand Paul to mean that the ego now, rather than being *controlled,* is to be *crucified.* He seems then to say that the crucified self will then be resurrected— but with *Christ* rather than *human ego* being its center and drive. And of course, the Christ who then "lives in me" is also the Christ who "gives himself," "empties himself," "denies himself," "takes the form of a servant," declines equality, and regularly subordinates himself—the Christ who is the very personification of anti-ego. And that is the "mind" of his we are to have in ourselves. It cannot be said that the Christian principle leaves the "self" dead: "whoever loses his life will *save* it," "the life I now live." However, it can be said that the "ego" is crucified, or lost, and that the self is raised with the anti-ego Christ in its place.

"But you can't ask people to crucify their own egos, ask the ego to crucify itself, as it were. That's suicide! And do it on the gamble there might be a 'resurrection'? That doesn't make any sense at all. And who would want to lose his ego in any case? That's all he's got, everything he is."

That's right! This Christian "extraordinary" is nothing that can be offered to the world as a superior alternative to its parity principle. It will make sense to and be a possibility only for those who already know Christ and are in him. For that matter, the suggestion never was that we crucify our own egos; it was that they be crucified *with him*. So all Christians have to offer the world is the gospel, Christ himself. But failing the acceptance of that, we have nothing to propose in the way of criticism of the parity principle or any superior ethical guidance. And above all, we have no right to demand that those who do not belong to Christ behave as though they did. No, our only quarrel is with *Christians* who understand no better than that the parity principle *is* the gospel and who thus betray their avowed rule of faith and practice.

It should be admitted, too, what Jesus, Paul, and, for that matter, any Christian knows—namely, that this business of death and resurrection is not as quick and easy as it might sound. Egos don't take that well to being crucified and staying crucified—nor to making room for *Christ* to live in me. And Paul would be the last to interpret his statement as a claim that, as a matter of personal, empirical fact, his own ego no longer lived at all but only Christ within him. No, presently, even with God's help, Christians can manage this death and resurrection only to a degree; they know the procedure will never be complete "until he comes." We believe, of course, that our truth of the gospel is vastly truer than the truth of the world; but we cannot claim to be living up to ours any better than the world is living up to its.

For the next step of our argument we need to realize that the New Testament conveniently summarizes this entire "voluntary subordination" package into one word: *agape*. Although we undoubtedly are oversimplifying a rather complex definition of terms, as far as it goes *eros* can be identified as "self-interested, ego-serving love" and *agape* as "self-forgetful, ego-denying love." This is why, in the New Testament, *agape* always comes "from above," must always have reference to *God*. No more than in the case of voluntary subordination can *agape* be recommended to the world as a form of love superior to the *eros* it has known. No, "in this is *agape,* not that we loved God (in our erotic, ego-serving way), but that he showed *agape* toward us (in the self-forgetful, us-remembering act of the Servant's death and resurrection)" [1 John 4:10, more or less]. "Have this mind among yourselves . . . " says nothing different from "Practice agape." And all of the New Testament teachings regarding *agape* belong under our rubric of voluntary subordination.

With this, we also get a new insight into Jesus' Second Commandment: "Love your neighbor as yourself." Most frequently this is read as a parity statement, "Love your neighbor on a par with yourself" — to which the party adds a rider, "And plainly, you need to take care of properly loving yourself before you will be capable of properly loving the neighbor (that's parity)."

The reading I now propose fits the text just as well as the parity interpretation does — and fits the overall context of the gospel a whole lot better: You take the love you naturally expend on yourself (which, by definition, must be *eros)* and expend it, instead, on the neighbor, for his sake (which, by definition, makes it *agape).* Or, to put it in different words, "If any man would come after me, let him deny himself."

And with that, we have two sorts of love — which are not quite synonymous with *eros* and *agape.* They are Paritous Love and Disparitous Love (I'm sorry, but I have to have adjectives which have not been invented until now).

Of course, not all *eros* recognizes parity as a limit; mostly it does not. Yet, all love that does seek parity is still a form of *eros* — controlled *eros* no less. Parity does undeniably include an element of self-interest: "I am ready to forego any thought of ego-dominance, but I demand the right of ego-parity; I will not be made subordinate." Paritous love is, accordingly, love between equals; it demands equality (in marriage, friendship, society, or wherever) as the necessary ground of true love. If it does not necessarily assume that the beloved is ready to reciprocate in love, it does assume that the very love of the lover will itself produce reciprocity (that's parity). To be loving is promoted as the best way to get oneself loved. In any case, this "mutuality," this "saluting your brethren only (or those you have reason to think will respond as brethren)," is the name of the game. And this is the highest form of love the world can understand or of which it will ever be capable.

Agape, on the other hand, is essentially a disparitous form of love; it assumes disparity at every turn. Even though its ultimate goal and hope is for universal reciprocity, that is no condition for its love. It is most quick to give itself where there is the least possibility of reciprocity. Its first and most fundamental disparity, of course, lies in the fact that it is God's love for us while we were yet sinners (sinning against *him*)—what chance of mutuality or reciprocity there?

But further: "If you love those who love you, what reward have you? . . . And if you salute only your brethren, what more are you doing than [the paritists of the world]?" (Matthew 5:46-47). The Old Testament *hesed* discussed in our Micah chapter is essentially disparitous in that it designates the faithfulness of one covenant partner even when the other is unfaithful. Likewise, New Testament *agape,* in being the love manifest on the cross, assumes a similar disparity. Again, the command that we love our enemies and those who despitefully use us speaks not simply of a lack of reciprocity but of negative reciprocity (and although often exegeted differently, scripture gives absolutely no guarantee that our love will convert enemies to friends). And finally, the notice of Jesus-love as being "to the end," or "unto death," indicates a love that continues in utter failure, in the most disparate of circumstances. So in this case as earlier, paritous love must be respected as the highest ideal of which the world is capable; yet there is no way Christian love can be seen as an equivalent.

Yet, not only "love" but most of the big terms of the gospel speak of disparity rather than parity: King, Lord, Master, Father, grace, mercy, forgiveness, judgment, sin, repentance, conversion, praise, confession, worship, and so on down the line. The Bible does include the great "equality" of which Kierkegaard spoke, but it can hardly be read as a manifesto of parity.

And just so, New Testament ethical counsel focuses upon the disparitous theme of voluntary subordination. The cross, of course, is made the paradigm. Jesus' washing the feet of his disciples may be the more pointed demonstration: "I have given you an example, that you also should do as I have done to you" (John 13:15). Likewise, all the teachings of *agape* and servanthood belong here. Then, more specifically, the scriptures ring with such phrases as these: "Love your neighbor as yourself." "Love your enemies." "Greater love has no man than this, that a man lay down his life." "Outdo one another in showing honor (in honor preferring one another)." "We who are strong ought to bear with the failings of the weak, and not to please ourselves; let each of us please his neighbor for his good, to edify him." "To have lawsuits at all with one another is defeat for you. Why not rather suffer wrong?" "Let no one seek his own good, but the good of his neighbor." "Love does not insist on its own way. Love bears all things." "You know the grace of our Lord Jesus Christ, that though he was rich, yet for your sake he became poor, so that by his poverty you might become rich." "We are glad when we are weak and you are strong." "Bear one another's burdens, and so fulfill the law of Christ." "Be subject to one another out of reverence for Christ." "In humility count others better than yourselves." "Even if I am to be poured as a libation upon the sacrificial offering of your faith, I am glad and rejoice with you all." "I rejoice in my sufferings for your sake." "If when you do right and suffer for it you take it patiently, you have God's approval. For to this you have been called, because Christ also suffered for you, leaving you an example, that you should follow in his steps." Here—and here only—lies the truly equitable humanism of Christianity.

Now granted, hidden in all this is something that *could* be identified as "parity." The ultimate goal of biblical ethics is that *everyone* "be subject to one another out of reverence for Christ" (and that's parity, of a sort). Yet, two considerations disallow this from being a form of the parity principle. In the first place, parity is not the conscious or immediate goal—subordination is. And whatever parity is finally achieved is a *gift* rather than being the product of any parity-seeking process in itself. Secondly, this Christian parity is the very opposite of the *upward* parity bent on asserting oneself *out* of subordination and into equality. Rather than pushing toward ego-equality at the ceiling of parity, scripture invites us all voluntarily to renounce ego *downward* to the equality of zero.

Obviously, Christianity's proposal is the much more radical of the two—so radical that the world must scorn it as foolish and impossible. And Christians would agree: it is entirely foolish and impossible—unless, from above, one has met and known the Sponsor and Resurrection-Capable Guarantor of the proposal.

Way back when, we interrupted our discussion of "justice"; now we can take it up again. We had said that the parity party's idea of justice is equal rights, equal opportunity, equal distribution of resources, etc. The biblical idea, on the other hand, is God's right way of getting things ordered as he considers right. And now we are in a position to say what the Bible means by that.

The right *way* of getting things right is what the righteous Judge did in giving his Son to be our Advocate, particularly in the judgment accomplished through his death and resurrection. (Markus Barth is entirely convincing in his argument that precisely here is where the gospel spots justice, justification, right-making, and salvation. Any attempt to define "justice" without referring to the death and resurrection of Jesus is not dealing with the New Testament concept.) The *state* of true rightness, then, is that obtaining when the "ego/*eros*/equality self" (the Triple E Self) is crucified with Christ to be raised with him as a "servant/*agape*/subordinating self" (the SAS Self). And although we can only approve the secular effort to achieve what the world calls "the just society" (that's parity), our rule of faith and practice tells us that the only "just society" truly deserving the name, or having any hope of becoming actual, is the body of Christ, the community of a servant people putting the interests of others above their own.

I am not able to discern any real distinction between "justice" and "liberation" except that of terminology. However, let me also state the case in terms of liberation. The theology of parity seeks to free us from the disparities of outward circumstance that oppress and subordinate us—doing this, of course, by moving us toward equality. Conversely, the biblical approach offers to loose us from enslavement to our own "ego/*eros*/equality selves." Political parity centers us on the self-interested liberation of being free *from* whatever we find inhibiting; Christianity on the self-forgetful liberation of being free *for* the service of God and neighbor. Here again, the biblical idea is much more the radical. The parity approach assumes that outward circumstance is all that needs to be changed and that human ego is fully competent to control itself in making those changes. The biblical approach assumes that the power of ego to control itself is very limited indeed and that it is only through changed, ego-denying people that God's love and power can be effective in changing the structures of the world. This way both cuts in at a much deeper level and makes much greater use of the help of God than does the parity approach.

Yet, it is when we move to "community" that the contrast becomes complete. In wanting to bring God (and Christ) into parity with man, the party is prohibiting the body from having a "head." And the Bible knows that a head is absolutely essential in giving any body its identity, unity, organization, and coordination. Yes, a head does imply "dominance"; but without dominance, no concept of "body" is even possible.

Just as seriously, the parity of subjective experience which claims ultimate truth as being that which is true *for me* — this undercuts the commonality of any objective truth that could bind us to one another or in which we might share. It makes for an individualistic atomism which is totally prohibitive of true community.

Then, regarding the Triple E Self over against the SAS Self, it is "self"-evident which is made for community. Servanthood, *Agape,* and Self-subordination do, in and of themselves, produce community. An SAS Self can't even be thought of outside community — any more than community can be thought of as constituted of anything other than SAS Selves. Triple E Selves, on the other hand, can never constitute true community. The thrust of ego and of *eros*-dominated, self-interested love are roadblocks rather than helps.

Competition rather than community is now the order of the day; one person's assertion toward parity inevitably leaves a wake of adversaries who feel their own equality threatened. And even the achievement of parity would make for a very unstable form of community. Once we ever get there (if we can even agree that we've arrived), there is no guarantee that the balance will hold. Instead of trust, there must be continual jockeying for position and the eagle-eyed suspicion that someone might be trying to put me down or himself up.

Where the SAS community can be at one in the knowledge that nothing can separate us from the *agape* of Christ, the Triple E Gang wants to be together only so they can watch each other in protecting their equal rights, their equal share of the pot. Although Christian community will produce the downward parity of each in honor preferring the other, the upward parity of the principle party will never produce anything like Christian community.

I admit it has taken me a while to catch up to what is probably the most basic difference between the biblical idea of justice and the secular tradition of parity-justice, what is the defect that makes parity constitutionally inadequate for the service of the gospel. Yet, it turns out to be an idea well worth waiting for. Biblical justice *includes* grace; parity-justice *excludes* it — it's as simple as that.

I sent an early draft of this chapter to *The Other Side* (no, not to heaven but to a very earthly magazine of Christian discipleship bearing that misleading name), asking whether they wanted me to make an article of any part of it. Friend and editor Mark Olson responded that they did; but he also opined, "I kind of think [is that any way for a literate editor to write?] that you're overlooking quite a few biblical texts that *do* talk of equality." And to back up his claim, he cited one, "If you have two coats, and your brother has none . . . "

Now I kind of think that Olson was kind of thinking that he was quoting Jesus. In fact, I was kind of thinking the same thing — until I located Luke 3:11 and discovered that the line belongs to John the Baptist and isn't quite as Olson quotes it, either. But no matter; I am quick to grant that this is something Jesus might just as likely have said (or something that could as well have been said anywhere in scripture). My interest, rather, is in showing that the statement belongs entirely to the biblical concept and has no hint of parity-justice about it.

Notice, first, that "Jesus" appeals to the person with two coats to practice the grace of *giving away* one of them. There is no hint either of his being critical of that person for having had two coats in the first place or of his citing any law of "parity" demanding that he give up one. And most decidedly he does not use the standard parity tactic of addressing the uncoated, "If you see a person with two coats and you have none, know that you have a right to one of his and would be justified in *taking* it if necessary — that's parity."

But more, I see some things in this incident that most people probably have overlooked. The person with the two coats was a *woman* (women have their right to be biblical characters, too, you know — that's parity). And she knew that, in the society of her day, the average male ownership was *three* coats. She was acutely aware as to where "parity" lies and was, in fact, on the way to try and acquire her equal-rights third coat when "Jesus" accosted her. And for him to suggest that she pass up her parity-rights and even forfeit them by giving away one of her hard-won *two* coats was about as unjust, oppressive, and sexist a demand as could be made. Why pick on her? Why didn't he talk to some of the truly rich, above-parity males who have three or four or more coats? (And why do we assume that the two-coater involved would necessarily be a rich person?)

Chapter Two: The fellow who was given a coat turned out to be not particularly grateful. Why should he be? After all, he hadn't received anything he did not rightly deserve; and he was still a long way from parity. Yet, next day, if Jesus had encountered *him,* it would be just like him to say, "If you see a cold child, give him your one coat." (That Jesus character has no appreciation at all of a person's right to get what he deserves. Nobody will ever get up to parity with him around.) But our man had different ideas. His new coat at least now gave him a start. If he would leave it at home and then talk the Welfare Department into coming through with the minimum one coat that society undeniably owes him, then he would at least be on a parity with the women. This certainly would not be to claim any more than simple justice.

The trouble, of course, is that, by the time he got his second coat, the women would have won their right to three. They then would have noticed that, if not quite the average, yet at least a great many men have *four* coats — and women, plainly, should have the right to equality not only with *some* men but with the best of them.

You see, being the sinful humans we are, the universal law of parity is this: the ceiling of parity always lies just a bit above where I am now. In theory, "parity control" sounds real good ("All I want is to be equal; I'm not asking for any special favors"). But in practice, it proves to be no ceiling at all — because no one will admit that he already is receiving justice. Each can find areas where he deserves better than he is getting—and right there is where each feels a holy obligation to see that justice gets done.

So it is my understanding that Jesus (with this assist from John the Baptist) comes precisely to knock the props out from under the worldly concept of parity-justice. As a previous chapter showed us, what the Bible calls "justice" is much more like "grace," much more akin to what we have called "downward parity." We are to forget all this business about upward parity and what I or anyone else *deserves*. If God were to deal with us on the basis of what we "deserve," we'd all go to hell. No, if you see someone in need, don't even raise the unanswerable parity question; just *give in grace*. And let the receiver also *receive in grace* (graciously) rather than claiming rights. Although "parity" is the best the world can think or do, it still marks the spirit of competition and ego-assertion which is of the devil.

I eventually came to realize that the fundamental weakness of parity-justice is not simply that it *overlooks* grace (which situation could be corrected with some good biblical teaching) but that it actually *precludes* grace. I tried a little experiment in one of my college classes; it was quite revealing.

Mentally draw for yourself a horizontal line representing the level of parity—which, of course, is also the level of "justice," "equal rights," "what I *deserve*," "fair treatment," or whatever. Of course, that line must be hypothetical in that we can never get it precisely defined. Yet, objectively, there does have to be such a level in there somewhere, it being the very standard to which parity-justice is dedicated. But any treatment I receive that falls below the line is "injustice," "oppression," "unfair treatment." However, consider that any treatment that comes *above* the line rightly must be qualified as "grace," the receiving of more than I deserve, of being treated better than I deserve.

Yet, the case is that we simply are not very good at doing an honest reading of our own charts. For the vast majority of us, I think, the true reading would have to be, "Well, I was poorly treated in this and this and this. But you know, these particular people on these particular occasions did much better by me than I would have had any right to expect. And in the balance, those graces offset these injustices to the point that I have no grounds for complaint. All things considered, I really have been treated very well."

My own conviction is that we all live by grace—by the grace of God, certainly, although we don't hear much about that these days, either in church or anywhere else. We also live by the grace we tender to each other. But the sad thing is that we do not, or will not, accept and credit grace for what it is. Quite the contrary, our tendency (our ego-assertive tendency) is to push that parity line clear up to the top of the chart. In consequence, we are acutely aware of how poorly we are treated (that is what "consciousness raising" is all about) and haven't even any means of recognizing treatment that is better than we deserve.

When someone reviews one of my books in a way that is manifestly unfair ("What did I ever do that people should have it in for me?"), I am very cognizant of the fact and deeply hurt. I nurture the memory of that injustice and hang on to it forever. But on the other hand, I know it is simply not possible for a book of mine to be reviewed as any better than it actually is. If the review is glowing, that only indicates that the book is as the review says, that a reviewer, for once, is telling the truth about it. And if that is the simple truth about the book, then it is also simple justice that the reviewer say so. As author, I am getting nothing that wasn't fully deserved. And because there is, thus, no such thing as a "grace" that could counterbalance my bad reviews, I still have grounds for my hurt and complaint—that's parity. As we have said, the concept of parity-justice is set up so as to preclude grace.

In class—where about half the students were black—we discussed Mohammed Ali as an example. The argument was vehement that in no way could his millions upon millions of dollars and tons of adulation be considered as marks of above-the-line grace that should have any bearing at all upon whatever below-the-line injustice he may have received as a young black. Very emphatically it was stated that anybody *deserves* anything he can get. In effect (although the class discussion did not get this far) there is no such thing as "grace." Indeed, grace would constitute a threat to the very operation of parity-justice. In the first place, to confess that I even need "grace" would be a weakness, a self-indictment betraying a low self-image. And what is even more serious, it would be giving away my one advantage, the image of "outraged innocence" which is the very basis for my right and demand to be treated better than I have been. The name of the game is to keep my "deserving level" as high as it can go.

And presently we have society set up to operate just this way. Now, with the exception of White Anglo-Saxon Well-To-Do Conservative Males [WAWCMs], anyone can identify with one oppressed minority or another. This, then, automatically qualifies him to claim his marks as all falling well below the line—without it even being necessary to document them from his personal history. For instance, "Women are a mistreated minority. I am a woman. Ergo, I am right to be angry about not being treated any better than I am."

Conversely the WAWCMs can now be made the scapegoats for all the injustice of the world. So, if blacks display anything that looks like racism, we are to know that, considering how they have been treated by the WAWCMs, their reaction is understandable and must be attributed to the WAWCMs rather than to themselves. If there are women who go into prostitution, it is only because the dear saintesses have been forced into it by the WAWCMs. If there is injustice anywhere in the world, it is the WAWCM United States Government that is behind it. If women were running things, we wouldn't have any more war (which, by the way, is about as sexist a statement as I've seen anywhere). I need to do a little more math before I get to "666," but there is no longer any mystery as to who is the Antichrist—the WAWCMs no less, because it obviously cannot be the deserving poor who constitute the rest of humanity.

What it comes to is that, in a world hell-bent for "justice," we don't find much of a witness to grace. We don't find much recognition of or gratitude for the grace we have received either from God or from others. We don't find much willingness to extend either our grace or God's to other people—particularly WAWCMs (best personified, perhaps, in Presidents Reagan or Nixon?). No, our passion for justice simply doesn't leave any room for grace.

So I put it to the class: "Girls, would you say you were treated differently from your brothers when you were growing up?" "You bet! We had to be in earlier at night. They got cars sooner. And so on and so on." "But can you think of any privileges you received that they didn't—such as more money for clothes, not having to earn your own way as soon, anything of that sort?" Sheepish grins. There you have our selective memories: we do very well at remembering injustices and don't recognize a grace when one blesses us.

"Can any of you recall occasions upon which your parents treated you considerably better than you deserved?" Sheepish grins all around.

"Have any of you, in a course, ever received better grades than you deserved?" Sheepish grins (of which we had a lot that day).

Being myself a very gracious grade-giver, I am particularly sensitive on this one. So let's talk about it for a little—with the understanding, first, that I by no means have in mind *all* college students and, second, that I am using them as a picture of the whole bunch of us rather than bringing any special charges. But, of course, the favorite tune of college students is, "We want to be treated as adults." And that is to say, "Let's establish our relationship on a basis of parity-justice; we will assume full responsibility for our own actions and expect the faculty to reciprocate by giving us precisely what we deserve."

However, just as soon as it comes to matters of shoddy class attendance, work that doesn't get done when it should, or examinations which (for very involved reasons) go bad—even though any of this, in a real parity relationship of secular employment, would lead to immediate dismissal, in college it is expected to lead to a suspension of the parity agreement. For years I sat on the Appeals Committee to which students apply for special privilege and exception to the rules. Ours could as well have been called the Committee of Grace: "No, you poor thing, you won't have to take the consequences of your action; we'll bend the rules to give you every possible opportunity to redeem yourself." College is very much a business of students talking "justice" even while accepting "grace."

Yet, the saddest aspect of the matter is the rather clear pattern that the student who is most in need of grace (because of his own irresponsibility), and thus the one who also receives the most grace, is generally the one least likely to recognize it as grace and confess it for what it is. He tends to come on, rather, as though it is the rules that were unjust in the first place—of all things, suggesting that people ought to attend class, do their assignments, or whatever. Yet, in this regard, consider that perhaps the greatest insult we can offer to God or to anyone else is to accept grace as though it were not grace but something that is ours by right.

But this is us all over. That race which most needs grace, which came into being through grace and continues each day only by virtue of it (I mean, of course, ours, the human race), is yet the very race most disinclined to render exhomologesis or to admit that we have ever received even as much as "justice." And obviously, never having received grace, we aren't about to extend any, either: "I'm for *justice*. In making myself what I am, I've had to work and even fight every step of the way up. I have never needed *grace*, wanted *grace*, or asked for *grace*. And I see no reason why I should be expected to extend grace to anyone now—there's no parity in that. I'm for justice."

My final question came after class was dismissed and the kids were on their way out of the room: "Do you think there are any feminists who could bring themselves to admit, who could afford to admit, that they have received much gracious, above-the-line treatment even from WAWCMs?"

In contrast to all this, our Old Testament chapter showed that, there, God's "justice" is much closer to "grace" than to the "demand your equal rights" that we commonly call "justice." And then, just above, we saw that all the New Testament teaching of servanthood, *agape*, and self-subordination does, rather, urge upon us a practice of justice that totally ignores the worldly ideal of parity and lives instead by what we could as well have called "grace." And to live by grace consists both in acknowledging the grace we all receive from God and from others and in our extending God's grace and our own to others.

In consequence, it strikes me that liberation theology, the peace and justice movement, the feminist movement—the whole parity idea—could use some New Testament plumblining and a great deal of rethinking.

In winding up this chapter, finally, I need to make clear what has been the point of the entire exercise. I have no intent of trying to drum all parity theology out of the Church of the Brethren (or any other church). It has been made clear enough that I consider it a very poor and unbiblical theology. However, even poor theologies have their rights. And I am not challenging the right of any group of Brethren to hold what theology they will. No, my only concern is with what the following *Conclusion* will call "honesty."

What bothers me is to have people pushing parity theology with one hand while, with the other, voting that a central commitment of the Church of the Brethren is to the New Testament as our rule of faith and practice. Why don't these people, rather, have the courage to join the mix, identify themselves, tell us what they stand for, and take the floor in defense of their own views? The other theologies and parties of the church do so. The conservatives, for instance, show no reluctance in letting it be known where they stand regarding the scriptures. So why won't the paritists argue (or at least vote) what they quite clearly believe, namely, that true Brethrenism is in no way dependent upon the acceptance of a biblical theology but can do as well or better upon the basis of the parity principle or some other form of modernism? The church would be much more honest and healthy if we had all our agendas out in the open where we could look at and deal with them.

Conclusion

Allow me here to try a wrap-up and conclusion for the book as a whole. It was only after it had been thought up and written I realized that the model for what I was doing was Soren Kierkegaard's *Attack Upon Christendom,* a deep-level critique of his church, the 19th-century Church of Denmark (Lutheran). The scale must be about right: my "attack" compares to Kierkegaard's as the Church of the Brethren compares to "Christendom."

However, I must confess that I have not had the heart to even try for the same sort of sharp wit, satire, and irony that Kierkegaard did. I am enough "into" the Church of the Brethren, and the Church of the Brethren is enough "into" me, that I haven't found much to smile about while saying what I felt simply *had* to be said.

But it is entirely proper that now, with me, the same questions be raised as were addressed to Kierkegaard in response to his attack: What is it you are after? What do you want to see happen in the church? What is your "program"? Why don't you state the concrete changes you have in mind and propose the steps by which they might be accomplished?

In the face of such questions, Kierkegaard denied that he even had a program, that he was thinking in terms of "reforms" that might be organized and carried through. And I'm with him all the way. I have no problem with the organizational goals and objectives of the denomination, am supporting them fully, and would not change anything there if I could. However, Kierkegaard maintained (and I am seconding his motion) that there are some matters —some very critical matters—that lie beyond the scope of, that simply are not amenable to, the manipulations of corporate planning and organizational technique. You cannot even trace, let alone direct, the winds of the Spirit, for example. And you cannot mold the faith of a church—a people—by legislating, enforcing, or goal-setting what they ought to believe.

So neither Kierkegaard nor I have a program to submit to the consideration of any General Boards, Annual Conferences, districts, or congregations. Earlier, I tried to make it abundantly clear that is *not* my program to encourage any Brethren to become carping critics of the church at large or of any specific leaders and teachers within it. *Negativism* will not produce *positive* results. You don't get exhomologesis by volunteering to confess *other people's* sins for them. *God* is not praised simply in pointing the finger at his *detractors*.

And most decidedly, it is not my program to encourage people to give up and leave the Church of the Brethren (or any other denomination). There is no way such a move can be figured to lead to God's name becoming *more* hallowed and his will for the church being *more truly* done.

So let me say again what I said at the outset: It is not my intention, not my program, that this matter of faith orientation be introduced into the organizational life of the church in the form of agenda items, conference queries, questionnaires, statistical studies, official reports, or goal statements. "Faith comes from what is heard" (Romans 10:17); and what is heard, that text goes on to specify, is "the preaching of Christ," not the findings of official boards and committees.

Even more strongly, it is not my program that we introduce disciplinary actions—investigating committees, creedal definitions, heresy trials, inquisitions, pastoral firings, or excommunications. Faith does not come from those things, either. Rather than building faith, such tactics only make people dishonest about what their faith actually is. It is not my program that the church's true believers organize to eliminate the false believers. Biblical faith calls for *each* believer to pray, "Help thou *my* unbelief."

Most strongly of all, it is not my program that the church meet the situation by passing new *resolutions*. The last thing in which I am interested is Annual Conference coming back to reaffirm: THE NEW TESTAMENT IS OUR RULE OF FAITH AND PRACTICE (in capital letters, note) accompanied by a rider reading, "And this time we really mean it." I would guess God has had about enough of that; and I doubt whether he has ever accepted church declarations as earnest money. No, we are in a situation where "words" avail nothing at all. Although God is too much of a gentleman to say it, "Shut up and get busy" is the only counsel appropriate for us.

So Kierkegaard said, "I don't have in mind any program of reform." And I say that I don't have in mind any program of reform. So, it was next put to Kierkegaard, "Then just what *are* you asking—what is it you want from the church?" And his was a one-word answer: "Honesty." All he was asking was that the church get honest about its own situation—anything more would come from that.

One reader of the manuscript urged me here to come on as a prophet, denouncing our sin, threatening doom, vigorously calling the church to repentance. But frankly, I don't feel in myself any of the confidence or authority of a prophet—nor do I particularly appreciate those who take it upon themselves to address the church so. Consequently, I am ready to go with Kierkegaard on this one, too.

Think about it, and you will realize there are two different ways we could go about getting honest. I would settle for either. We could confess, "It is true that, although we *say* the New Testament is our rule of faith and practice, neither our faith nor our practice indicate that actually to be the case. What we presently call our 'Brethrenism' does not give evidence of being rooted in the heart and core of what Brethrenism has always represented. Our actions, our worship, our life—none reflect the Bible's passionate zeal that, above all else, *God's* name be hallowed." And then, under the embarrassment of that admission, we just might repent and seek God's help in becoming the church we already say we are.

That is one way to go. The other way to get honest is to say, "It is true that we are not in any serious way taking the New Testament as our rule of faith and practice. Let us then, officially, by Conference action, retract that statement, reject the old chart, and redefine Brethrenism in a way that *does* square with the church we actually are, with what we actually are believing and doing."

Obviously, the first alternative would be my choice; but it is not my place to demand and insist upon it. Yet, in all seriousness, I have to say I would prefer the second over simply continuing as we are, saying we are one thing while actually being another. My feeling is that God recognizes and values *honesty,* even if it be the honest admission that we have chosen another lover (our own humanity) and are rejecting him.